S0-BAZ-105

INSTALLATION SERVICES THAT INSPIRE

INSTALLATION SERVICES THAT INSPIRE

Impressive
programs for your
church or organization

Leila T. Ammerman

BROADMAN PRESS
Nashville, Tennessee

© Copyright 1982 • Broadman Press
All rights reserved.
4236-16
ISBN: 0-8054-3616-2

Dewey Decimal Classification: 268.7
Subject heading(s): INSTALLATION SERVICES
Library of Congress Catalog Card Number: 81-67371
Printed in the United States of America

Contents

General Introduction

The planning of an installation service for the members of the church staff, or for officers who are elected to serve in a church or community organization, is exceedingly important because such a service impresses upon the congregation or membership the solemn responsibility of the relationship which they have undertaken.

This book is a resource planned to assist those who conduct such installation services. It would be helpful on the shelf of every church library, and would serve the community on the public library shelf as well.

The dedication of new church equipment tends to make all who are involved view that equipment as sacred to the service of God, and so it is set apart from things of the world and is to be used with reverence.

The purpose of this book is to make available various installation or dedication services which will be meaningful in making plans and putting together formal, printed programs.

These services will be outlined so they may be used completely as planned, or any portions thereof may be selected and utilized in planning the service.

There is a great variety of services included in this volume. There are long, formal, involved, and complete services, which lend themselves to the setting up of a printed program. Some are planned using various forceful symbols and visual aids. There are also simple, brief, formal, and informal services which will be adequate for the small church or organization, and for those times when the installation service is planned as part of the service or program.

Some services are planned so they may be conducted to install a large slate of officers in a big church. Even those services may be easily adapted, leaving out those officers not needed and lending themselves to the smallest of organizations.

In a book this size, appropriate Scripture verses and passages for Scripture lessons may obviously be used in several services. The Scripture throughout is taken from the King James Version.

Although this book is planned primarily for those responsible for installations in church work, there is also a section including installations to be used for veteran's, civic, and social organizations, as needed.

I would suggest that in using long services with printed programs, the various parts of the service be given to visiting officials, who might then choose whether or not to use the printed suggestions.

In the brief services, officials of the church or officers of the organization might lead the various parts of the service.

It is my hope that this book will fill a definite need, and that it may be genuinely helpful to many churches and organizations.

LEILA T. AMMERMAN

PART 1
AREA OF CHURCH MINISTRY

As we consider the area of church ministry, we are impressed with the thought that any ceremony or service which can make events and relationships more meaningful are well worth the time we give to them.

When a new minister comes to the congregation of a church, it is hopefully the beginning of a very unique relationship, based on mutual love, respect, and trust.

It is most fitting that a formal service of installation be planned, so that the solemn responsibilities assumed by all parties to the agreement may be emphasized and soberly accepted by all.

A new minister may approach the task of undertaking the spiritual leadership of a new congregation with many feelings of inadequacy. But he knows that if he seriously seeks God's guidance, and undergirds his work with honest prayer, he will find the divine help he needs to carry through his mission.

The congregation should accept the new minister with love, and a determination to be helpful and supportive of his ministry. It takes all the various groups and organizations of the church, as well as the individual members working together, to see that the church is the growing edge of the kingdom of God.

In Paul's letter to the Ephesian church we read: "Now therefore ye are no more strangers and foreigners, but fellow-citizens with the saints, and of the household of God. And are built upon the foundation of the apostles and prophets, Jesus Christ himself being the chief corner stone; In whom all the building fitly framed together groweth unto an holy temple in the Lord: In whom ye also are builded together for an habitation of God through the Spirit" (Eph. 2:19-21).

This is our hope and prayer for the relationships that are formed that they may upbuild themselves in love.

This area of church ministry includes the installation of new ministers and associate ministers; the installation or ordination of new deacons, (elders, stewards, vestrymen, etc.); the dedication of new communion ware and new pulpit furniture.

The services may be adapted for printed programs (leaving out the notes for guest speakers). Every one is planned so that all or any parts of the services may be used.

May these services serve to enrich our lives, and consecrate our solemn assemblies.

Installing the New Minister

Service 1

Name of Church
Name of Denomination
City and State
A Service of Installation
for
Name of New Minister
Time and Date

Staff Member or Other Church Leader Presiding

An Act of Reverence

Prelude
Call to Worship:

"O come, let us worship and bow down: let us kneel before the Lord our maker. For he is our God; and we are the people of his pasture, and the sheep of his hand" (Ps. 95:6-7).

Let us come into this place in this holy hour in an attitude of worship and adoration of our God. May this service be undergirded by our individual and collective prayers.

Hymn: "I Love to Tell the Story"
Invocation and the Lord's Prayer:

Our Father, we would invoke thy presence, so that the things we do and say here may be acceptable in thy sight. Widen our hearts with thy love, and let us truly worship thee as we pray together the prayer that Jesus taught us:

"Our Father which art in heaven, Hallowed be thy name. Thy kingdom come. Thy will be done in earth, as it is in heaven. Give us this day our daily bread. And forgive us our debts, as we forgive our

11

debtors. And lead us not into temptation, but deliver us from evil: For thine is the kingdom, and the power, and the glory, for ever. Amen'' (Matt. 6:9-13).

An Act of Fellowship

Hymn: "In Christ There Is No East or West"
Scripture Lesson: 2 Corinthians 5:20 to 6:13
Greetings: From the Community (by mayor or other official)
From Sister Churches (by minister or other official)
From the Congregation (by presiding officer)

Let me use the words of the apostle Paul to welcome you this day. We would particularly greet our honored guests, our new minister, and the congregation of this church.

"Grace be unto you, and peace from God our Father, and from the Lord Jesus Christ. I thank my God always on your behalf, for the grace of God which is given you by Jesus Christ. That in every thing ye are enriched by him, in all utterance, and in all knowledge; Even as the testimony of Christ was confirmed in you; So that ye come behind in no gift; waiting for the coming of our Lord Jesus Christ: Who shall also confirm you unto the end, that ye may be blameless in the day of our Lord Jesus Christ. God is faithful, by whom ye were called unto the fellowship of his Son Jesus Christ our Lord'' (1 Cor. 1:3-9).

As the representative of this congregation, I greet you all and ask that our God will bless this day and the relationship into which we are about to enter. Amen.

An Act of Renewal

Anthem or *Solo:* The Lord's Prayer—Malotte
The Message of Challenge: Guest of Honor

Let Him Minister

A spiritual leader comes by many names—"Preacher," "Evangelist," "Minister," "Pastor," and all these are descriptive terms. All may be applied to the spiritual leader of a congregation.

The minister comes to a congregation to carry many responsibilities. But the congregation, the church leadership, and the members, have responsibilities, too.

The minister must be free to express the Word of God, as God gives him insight to see it. The minister is responsible to God, but so is the congregation.

Remember that the ninety and nine should not demand all of the minister's time—there must also be time to seek those who are lost.

Jesus was criticized by the Pharisees because he ate with and spent time with publicans and sinners. Was it not they whom God sent him to save? Let your minister be an evangelist to the lost. Let him be the preacher of God's Word.

Let him be your minister, serving all the congregation. Let him be your pastor, sharing with you both your joys and your sorrows. Let him be the spiritual leader of your church!

Hymn: "Have Thine Own Way, Lord"

Offering:

An Act of Installation
The Solemn Covenant

Presiding Chairman: In the name of our Lord Jesus Christ, who is the head of this church, we are met here this day to install _____ _____ as pastor of our congregation. This solemn occasion involves mutual trust and obligations, and under God we must unite in affirming our intent to make this relationship one which upbuilds the church of our Master and helps us to grow spiritually as we work together in harmony and fellowship.

Will the pastor to be installed stand before us and make his declaration?

Pastor: Willingly do I reaffirm my ordination vows. I believe that Jesus is the Christ, the Son of the living God, and I accept him as my Savior and my Lord. It is my sincere desire to devote my life to the preaching of God's Word and the serving of God's children. I would live so that I may bring honor to the gospel which I preach. I will fulfill to my utmost ability the office of a good minister of Jesus Christ.

Presiding Chairman: Will the representatives of various areas of church work come before us to make their pledges to the new minister?

Vice Chairman (Deacons, Elders, etc.):   I would pledge the full cooperation of our leaderhip to _____ our new minister. We will try to work together in full harmony, as the family of God, and to this we pledge ourselves. In the Book of Hebrews, we read:

"For this is the covenant that I will make with the house of Israel after those days, saith the Lord; I will put my laws into their mind, and write them in their hearts: and I will be to them a God and they shall be to me a people: And they shall not teach every man his neighbor, and every man his brother, saying, Know the Lord: for all shall know me, from the least to the greatest. For I will be merciful to their unrighteousness, and their sins and their iniquities will I remember no more (Heb. 8:10-12).

May our relationship be such that we may all grow in our knowledge of God and his kingdom.

Sunday School Superintendent (Director):   In the field of Christian education, we, the officers and teachers of the Sunday School, pledge ourselves to work together for growth in grace and the knowledge of our Lord and Savior, Jesus Christ. The people of our congregation are precious in the sight of our Lord, and we pledge that we will be mindful of the great responsibilities we share together, to bring them all to a fuller knowledge of God.

Presidents of Women's and Men's Organizations: We would pledge that our fellowship will be one of joy and peace together. In the First Epistle of John we read:

"That which we have seen and heard declare we unto you, that ye also may have fellowship with us: and truly our fellowship is with the Father, and with his Son Jesus Christ. And these things write we unto you, that your joy may be full" (1:3-4).

Together may we work to upbuild our church.

Head of Youth Organization: I have come to speak on behalf of the youth of our church. We welcome our new minister, and we pledge our full cooperation in the work he seeks to do here. In the Book of Job we read:

"I said, Days should speak, and multitude of years should teach wisdom. But there is a spirit in man: and the inspiration of the Almighty giveth them understanding'' (32:7-8).

We, the youth of the church, ask that God will grant us understanding, and that we may be a help to our minister in his service for God.

Presiding Chairman: Will the congregation please stand and repeat the vow of covenant in your bulletin?

Congregation: (In unison)

We solemnly affirm our membership in Christ's church and our fellowship in this congregation. We renew our vows of faith to our Lord Jesus Christ and our allegiance to his church. We covenant to cooperate with our new pastor to have fellowship in the family of God, and to extend the gospel in its purity and power in this community, and to our utmost ability, around the world. We pledge to give our pastor our love and support in the work of God which he has vowed to perform. So help us, God.

Prayer of Installation:

Eternal and Almighty God, who was, and is, and for ever shall be, we thank thee that thou hast brought us to this day in the life of our church. We are here together in thy presence, the minister and the congregation. We know that unless thou dost help to build thy church, we will labor in vain to build it. We beg that thou wilt look with lovingkindness upon us this day, and upon this service. Wilt thou richly bless our church and our new pastor, and may our relationship be loving and lasting, each upbuilding the other, that thy word may be spread in this community, and in thy world. Like Barnabas, may we be encouragers of this, thy servant and our new minister. May he be endowed with thy spirit, filled with thy peace and joy, and inspired by thy wisdom. We offer this prayer in the name of our Lord and Savior, Jesus Christ. Amen.

The Pronouncement: (by presiding chairman)

In the name of our Lord and Savior Jesus Christ, we hereby pronounce that you, _____, are duly installed as the pastor of this congregation. We commend you to the grace and love of God in the discharge of all the responsibilities of the office to which God and this congregation have called you. May we together be abundantly blessed in our joint worship and service of God. As representative of the congregation, I give you the right hand of fellowship.

Greetings from Honored Guests
Hymn: "Blest Be the Tie That Binds"
Benediction: (by newly installed minister)

Fellowship hour or reception to follow

Installing the New Minister

Service 2

Name of Church
Name of Denomination
City and State
A Service of Installation
for
Name of New Minister
Time and Date

Church Leader Presiding

Moment of Worship

Prelude:
Call to Worship:

"Praise ye the Lord. Praise God in his sanctuary: praise him in the firmament of his power. Praise him for his mighty acts: praise him according to his excellent greatness!" (Ps. 150:1-2).

"Let every thing that hath breath praise the Lord. Praise ye the Lord" (v. 6).

Hymn: "Joyful, Joyful We Adore Thee"
Invocation and the Lord's Prayer:

Eternal God and loving Father, we bow before thee in reverence and praise. We beg that thou wilt look down upon us thy servants, and this solemn occasion, and bless us and bless this day. Bring us close to each other and to thee in the bonds of thy holy love. Help us work and grow spiritually as we work together to build thy kingdom in this community, and in this world. We know that thou lovest the world and thy own Son was sent to redeem us and to teach us the way to live together in love. May we follow the path of our Lord and Master, Jesus the Christ, is our prayer this day. Now may we pray together the prayer he taught us, saying:

"Our Father, which art in heaven, Hallowed be thy name. Thy kingdom come. Thy will be done in earth, as it is in heaven. Give us this day our daily bread. And forgive us our debts, as we forgive our debtors. And lead us not into temptation, but deliver us from evil: For thine is the kingdom, and the power, and the glory, for ever. Amen" (Matt. 6:9*b*-13).

Moments of Friendship

Hymn: "What a Friend We Have in Jesus"
Scripture Lesson: 1 Corinthians 3:1-9
Greetings: From the Community: (by mayor or other official)
From Sister Churches: (by minister or other official)
From the Congregation: (by representative)

I come before you this day as the representative of the congregation. We now together enter into a joyous yet solemn relationship, in which each of us must pledge to do his part. Our new minister cannot perform his ministry unless we, the congregation, stand behind him and support him with our time, our money, and our love. As the official representative of the congregation, I hereby pledge that we will strive to be helpful, not holding back; that we will offer our friendship, without reserve; that we will be often in prayer for him and for the good of the church. In the First Epistle of John we read:

"Beloved, let us love one another: for love is of God; and every one that loveth is born of God, and knoweth God. He that loveth not

17

knoweth not God; for God is love. In this was manifested the love of God toward us, because that God sent his only begotten Son into the world, that we might live through him. Herein is love, not that we loved God, but that he loved us, and sent his Son to be the propitiation for our sins. Beloved, if God so loved us, we ought also to love one another. No man hath seen God at any time. If we love one another, God dwelleth in us, and his love is perfected in us" (1 John 4:7-12).

This, we pray, will be a loving relationship. Amen.

Moments of Challenge

Anthem or *Solo:* "God So Loved the World"—Stainer
The Message: By Guest of Honor

Partners with God

The Scripture reading said: "We are labourers together with God." Indeed, the relationship we enter into is a partnership. God is the senior partner. The minister and the congregation are the junior partners. A partnership requires joint possession of a common interest. It is the purpose of the junior partners to carry out the will of the senior partner—the will of God. Our task is to express God's love for all mankind, to serve our fellowman, wherever he may be. To lead all men to the good news of the gospel of Jesus Christ. Together—as partners with God—we can do this!
Hymn: "Lord, Speak to Me that I May Speak"
Offering:

Moments of Consecration

Presiding Chairman: In the name of God, our senior partner, and his Son Jesus Christ, our Redeemer and Guide, we are met this day to install _____ as pastor of _____ _____ Church in _____. As junior partners, we pledge ourselves to uphold the work of the church, supporting our new minister in his effort to lead us in spiritual growth, and in doing the work of God; in learning to love all mankind, and in spreading the good news of the gospel of Jesus

Christ. To these ends we jointly pledge ourselves. Will the pastor to be installed please stand and make his declaration?

Pastor: Willingly and gladly I, _____, do hereby reaffirm my ordination vow. I believe with all my heart that Jesus is the Christ, the Son of the living God, and I have accepted him as my Savior, Redeemer, and Lord. I will study the Holy Bible, that I may understand God's will. I will spend much time in prayer, that I may understand God's love. I will strive to keep my private and public life above reproach, that I may bring honor to this church and to God. I will try to be a good minister to all the people, and a true spiritual leader, with God's help. Amen.

Presiding Chairman: Will the representatives of various areas of church work now stand to give their pledges of support for our new minister?

Vice Chairman: I do solemnly vow and affirm that we of the church leadership of _____ Church will support and assist our new pastor, _____, in the work of the church. We will pray for him and for our church, and we will give of our time and our money that the kingdom of God may be advanced both in our community and around the world. And we ask God's blessing upon us all who are fellow workmen for God in Jesus' name. Amen.

Sunday School Superintendent (Director): We of the Sunday School realize that study is an important element in Christian growth. I speak for the Sunday School staff and teachers, when I pledge that we will study, teach, and learn, so that the light of God's word may shine into all the dark corners of the globe; that the gospel of Jesus Christ may be spread ever farther in our own community and throughout the world.

Presidents of Men's and Women's Organizations: (In unison)
We, the presidents of the men's and women's organizations of the church, pledge that we will be active and helpful in church work. Jesus said: "And I, if I be lifted up from the earth, will draw all men unto me" (John 12:32). It shall be our task to lift Christ in our church and in our lives, and we will strive ever to do this.

President of Youth Organization: Youth are important, too. I represent the youth of our church, and I want to welcome our new pastor on their behalf. We pledge that we will try to be cooperative in the

19

programs that he plans for the church, and we will try to follow on the paths of spiritual growth where he leads the way. We would serve Jesus and the church in any way we can. We cannot do everything, but we can do something. And what we can do, we will do.

Presiding Chairman: Will the congregation please rise and repeat the pledge of partnership printed in the bulletin, in unison?

Congregation: We solemnly vow that we are members of Christ's church, and that we have fellowship with this congregation. We pledge ourselves to be junior partners in the work of the church. We will be faithful to the mission God has given us, to spread the good news of the gospel of Jesus Christ, and to feed and serve his people wherever there is need. We will respect and love our pastor, and give him freedom to preach the Word as God gives him unction. We will try to the best of our ability to be good fellow workers with Christ. So help us God!

Prayer of Installation: God our Father, and the Father of our Lord Jesus Christ, we come to thee humbly asking that thou wilt bless this day and this service. Let thy blessing fall upon this church, and our new minister, that we may truly serve thee. We remember how we have read that whenever Moses held up his hands, Israel prevailed against her enemies. When he lowered his hands, the battle went against Israel. And so Aaron and Hur held up his hands, one on either side, so that Israel should prevail. Do thou, our God, help us to remember to hold up the hands of our minister, so that together we may do great things for thee. This is our prayer this day as we pray that thou wilt surely install _____ in our hearts as well as in our church. For we ask this of thee humbly in Jesus' name. Amen.

Pronouncement: (by presiding chairman)

In the name of our Lord and Savior Jesus Christ, and in behalf of this congregation, I now pronounce you _____ duly installed as pastor of _____ Church at _____. Together as partners, God, the people, and the minister, we will work harmoniously together to advance the cause of the kingdom of God on earth. May you _____ be blessed in the work with us which you have undertaken. As the representative of the congregation, I now give you the right hand of fellowship.

The Honored Guests Congratulate the Minister
Hymn: "God Be with You Till We Meet Again"
Benediction: By the newly installed minister.
Postlude:

Fellowship hour or reception will follow.

Installing the New Minister

Service 3

Name of Church
Name of Denomination
City and State
for
Name of New Minister
Time and Date

Church Leader Presiding

Prelude
Call to Worship and Invocation Prayer:

"For this cause I bow my knees unto the Father of our Lord Jesus Christ,
Of whom the whole family in heaven and earth is named, That he would grant you, according to the riches of his glory, to be strengthened with might by his Spirit in the inner man; That Christ may dwell in your hearts by faith, that ye, being rooted and grounded in love,

May be able to comprehend with all saints what is the breadth, and length, and depth, and height; And to know the love of Christ, which passeth knowledge, that ye might be filled with all the fulness of God" (Eph. 3:14-19).

Will you bow and pray with me?

Almighty God and everlasting Father, we bow before thee this day, asking that thou wilt graciously bless us with thy presence on this joyous occasion. Bless this new relationship between minister and people, and may we mutually upbuild each other in the love and knowledge of Jesus Christ our Lord, for this we ask in his name. Amen.

Hymn: "Rise Up, O Men of God"
Scripture Lesson: Isaiah 6:1-8
General Prayer and the Lord's Prayer:

Creator God and Father of all living, we come to praise thee, adore thee, and worship thee. Thou hast been our God and our guide through all generations, and we know that thou wilt be with us in all our troubles and our joys. Wilt thou remember all thy children: heal the sick, comfort the afflicted, and care for those in need. Enrich our joy in this time when we begin a new era in our church. We believe that thou hast led us in forming these new ties of love and brotherhood, and we pray that together we may advance thy kingdom. Wilt thou hear us as we pray the prayer that Jesus taught us, saying:

"Our Father which art in heaven, Hallowed be thy name. Thy kingdom come. Thy will be done in earth, as it is in heaven. Give us this day our daily bread. And forgive us our debts, as we forgive our debtors. And lead us not into temptation, but deliver us from evil: for thine is the kingdom, and the power, and the glory, for ever. Amen" (Matt. 6:9-13).

Hymn: "I Would Be True"
Greetings: (The presiding chairman should introduce each, and all should remain till all have brought greetings.)

From the Congregation—by representative from the deacons
I represent our congregation to bring greetings to our new minister, _____. I also bring greetings to our honored guests, and all who have gathered here for this happy occasion. We are glad

you came, and we hope you will receive a blessing as we worship together.

From the Community—(by the mayor or other official)

From Sister Churches—(by representative)

The Message: *Willingness to Serve*—By Honored Guest
(Notes which may be helpful)

God raises up men in each generation to lead his church.

Every congregation owes a debt to each of its preachers, and each has had his own contribution to make to the total life of the church.

As the new minister undertakes the task of leading the church, he will need the help of every member to achieve the high goals that may be reached by joint, sustained effort.

Your minister said. "Here am I [Lord]; send me."

Will you be willing, when there is a task you can do, to call out to him: "Here am I; send me."

Offering:

Anthem or *Special Music:* "My Task"—Ashford

Presiding Chairman: *The Solemn Vows*

Will our new minister, _____, come forward to make his vow?

Minister: I, _____, do solemnly vow and covenant to be a faithful minister of our Lord, Jesus Christ. I will strive to lead a pure life in private and in public, and so fulfill my ordination vows. I reaffirm my belief that Jesus is the Christ, the Son of the living God, and I have accepted him as my personal Lord and Savior. I will preach the word as God gives me guidance, and I will be a pastor to this congregation, to nurture them in the truth of the Holy Scriptures. God helping me, I will do my best.

Presiding Chairman: Will the congregation please rise and repeat after me their vow?

Congregation: (In unison)

We, the congregation of _____ Church, do solemnly vow that we will give our support to our new minister, _____. We will try to give him time for study and for prayer and for his personal life. We will support his efforts to win souls to Christ, and we will work to build up the church and to follow in the ways our minister leads. We will be loving and understanding with each other, and so fulfill the law of Christ. We now affirm this solemn vow in God's sight.

Presiding Chairman: *The Pronouncement*

I now pronounce you, _____, duly installed as minister of the _____ Church. May God richly bless this ministry.

Hymn: "Lord, Dismiss Us with Thy Blessing"

Benediction: By the newly installed minister

Fellowship hour or reception to follow

Installing the New Associate Minister

Service 1

Name of Church
Name of Denomination
City and State
A Service of Installation
for
Name of Associate Minister
Time and Date

Senior Minister Presiding

Together in Worship

Prelude
Call to Worship:

"Kings of the earth, and all people; princes, and all judges of the earth: Both young men, and maidens; old men, and children: Let them praise the name of the Lord: for his name alone is excellent; his glory is above the earth and heaven. He also exalteth the horn of his people, the praise of all his saints: even of the children of Israel, a people near unto him. Praise ye the Lord'' (Ps. 148:11-14).

Hymn of Praise: "Holy, Holy, Holy, Lord God Almighty"
Invocation Prayer:
Eternal God and everlasting Father, we come to thee this day, and we beg that thou wilt bless this service, and the vows that we take to brotherhood and fellowship with each other. May thy presence be here with us in this house, and may we feel thy love and concern for us, thy children. We ask a special blessing as we begin our worship, and may it be meaningful to us all. For we ask it in the name of thy Son Jesus, our Lord. Amen.

Together in Fellowship

Hymn: "Take My Life, and Let It Be"
Scripture Lesson: Romans 8:27-39
Anthem or Special Music: "No Greater Love"—Peterson
Greetings: The senior minister greets his new associate minister, any guests who may be present, and the congregation.

Together in Love

The Message:
(Notes that may be helpful.)
Together is a very beautiful word, and should be used often by Christians.

Together in our work, together in our study, together in prayer, together in love.

Our Scripture lesson assured us that nothing can separate us from the love of God. Nothing should ever separate us from the love of our brother.

In 1 John we find these words: "He that loveth not his brother whom he hath seen, how can he love God whom he hath not seen?" (1 John 4:20*b*).
Offering:

Together in Dedication

Senior Minister: Will our new associate minister, _____
_____, please rise and stand before us to repeat his vow?

I, _____, as senior minister of this church welcome you as our new associate minister. We offer you a great challenge, to help lead us all in the pathways of spiritual growth, and to help us in our study of God's Holy Word and in our development in our prayer life.

We give our hands and our hearts to you in warm Christian fellowship.

We challenge you with words from the Ephesian letter "That Christ may dwell in your hearts by faith; that ye, being rooted and grounded in love, May be able to comprehend with all saints what is the breadth, and length, and depth, and height; And to know the love of Christ, which passeth knowledge, that ye might be filled with all the fulness of God" (Eph. 3:17-19). Now will you repeat your vow of dedication?

Associate Minister: I, _____, hereby rededicate myself to my vow to serve our Lord and Savior, Jesus Christ. I will strive to express in my private life as well as in my public actions the love of God which is in Christ Jesus, my Lord. As told once in the story of Moses:

"And it came to pass, when Moses held up his hand, that Israel prevailed: and when he let down his hand, Amalek prevailed. But Moses' hands were heavy; and they took a stone, and put it under him, and he sat thereon; and Aaron and Hur stayed up his hands, the one on the one side and the other on the other side; and his hands were steady until the going down of the sun" (Ex. 17:11-12).

This will be my task: to stand beside your pastor, and hold up his hands, so that the kingdom of God shall be advanced in this community, and the Word of God shall be taught and loved in this church. I solemnly dedicate myself to carry out this vow, with God's help.

Senior Minister: Will the congregation now rise and repeat the vow printed in the bulletin?

Congregation: (In unison)

We, the congregation of _____ Church now covenant and pledge that we will uphold the work of the kingdom of God, and support these, our ministers, in their work for that kingdom. We will give of our time, our work and our money, and we will build the fellowship of this church that together we may grow in the understanding of God's will. This we will do, so help us God!

Senior Minister: The Pronouncement

I now declare that you have been duly installed as associate minister of this congregation, and I ask God's blessing upon you. Amen.

Hymn: "Lord, Speak to Me That I May Speak"

Senior Minister: Will you now pronounce our benediction?

Associate Minister:

"The Lord watch between me and thee, when we are absent one from another (Gen. 31:49*b*).

"The Lord bless thee and keep thee: The Lord make his face to shine upon thee, and be gracious unto thee: The Lord lift up his countenance upon thee, and give thee peace" (Num. 6:24-26). Amen.

Fellowship hour or reception to follow

Installing the New Associate Minister

Service 2

Name of Church
Name of Denomination
City and State
A Service of Installation
for
Name of Associate Minister
Time and Date

Senior Minister Presiding

Adoration

Prelude
Call to Worship:

> "Seek ye the Lord while he may be found, call ye upon him while he is near: Let the wicked forsake his way, and the unrighteous man his thoughts: and let him return unto the Lord, and he will have mercy upon him; and to our God, for he will abundantly pardon. For my thoughts are not your thoughts, neither are your ways my ways, saith the Lord" (Isa. 55:6-8).

Hymn of Praise: "When Morning Gilds the Skies"
Invocation Prayer:

> Our God, the source of all life, all strength, all power, and all love, we ask that thou wilt be with us in this hour. Thou hast been our dwelling place for all generations, and we bow before thee in adoration. Bless this occasion that it may be worthy in thy sight, and may the relationships we forge this day be such that they will upbuild thy church. Let us now pray together the prayer that Jesus taught us, saying:

> "Our Father, which art in heaven, Hallowed be thy name.
> Thy kingdom come. Thy will be done in earth, as it is in heaven.
> Give us this day our daily bread.

> And forgive us our debts, as we forgive our debtors. And lead us not into temptation, but deliver us from evil: For thine is the kingdom, and the power, and the glory for ever. Amen" (Matt. 6:9-13).

Anthem or Special Music: "It Took a Miracle"—Peterson

Aspiration

Scripture Lesson: 2 Timothy 4:1-5
Greetings: The senior minister formally welcomes the new associate minister, greets the guests who may be present, and welcomes the congregation.
Hymn "O Master, Let Me Walk with Thee"
Pastoral Prayer:

> Omnipotent and Almighty God, we come to thee, aspiring to live ever more closely in thy presence and thy love. We seek thy mercy

for all thy wandering children, for we have all sinned against thee, and all fall short of the glory of God. We pray that thou wilt touch the ill with thy healing hand; give to those who mourn the comfort of thy love, and the knowledge of thy near presence. Grant to all who seek, visions of thy high calling to deep purpose and abundant life. May thy rich blessing be upon this day, upon us who worship here together, and especially upon this, thy son, our new associate, and the relationship we here now forge in thy sight. Let all that we do be done in the name and nature of Jesus, for in his name we pray. Amen.

Inspiration

The Message: Be Urgent in Season
(Notes which may be helpful)

A "coasting" Christianity cannot overcome a "crusading" paganism.

If you chose, would you live in ancient Greece, with war, bribery, murder, population explosion—new babies laid outside the cities to die of exposure?

Would you live in the middle ages, when in 1793 it was a death offense to show mercy to an enemy, even a child?

Would you live in the days of Indian raids, with your gun always handy to kill?

We are chosen to be here to meet the difficulties of these days, with God's help, and to lead his people to ever higher paths.

We must be urgent in season.

Preach the Word.

The power was always in Niagara, but only when men learned to harness it, was it useful to them.

Grant us wisdom and courage to find and use the power God has placed in our world, and to use it for good.

Hymn: "Dear Lord and Father of Mankind"
Offering:

Senior Minister: Will _____ , our new associate minister, now stand before us to repeat the vows of dedication? Do you, _____ , willingly undertake to serve as associate minister of the _____ Church, and do you vow to cheerfully accept the challenge to serve our Lord Jesus Christ in this community?

Associate Minister: I do.

Senior Minister: Do you further promise to be faithful to your ordination vows, to take Jesus as your Lord and Master, and to further the work of the church?

Associate Minister: I do.

Senior Minister: Do you covenant to lead a Christian life, in public and in private, that you may be an example to the congregation, and a strong help to our ministry?

Associate Minister: I do, so help me God!

Senior Minister: Will the congregation please rise, and read responsively with me?

Senior Minister: "For as we have many members in one body, and all members have not the same office:

People: "So we, being many, are one body in Christ, and every one members one of another.

Senior Minister: "Having then gifts differing according to the grace that is given to us, whether prophecy, let us prophesy according to the proportion of faith;

People: "Or ministry, let us wait on our ministering:

Senior Minister: "Or he that teacheth, on teaching;

People: "Or he that exhorteth, on exhortation:

Senior Minister: "He that giveth, let him do it with simplicity;

People: "He that ruleth, with diligence.

Senior Minister: "He that sheweth mercy, with cheerfulness.

People: "Let love be without dissimulation. Abhor that which is evil; cleave to that which is good" (Rom. 12:4-9).

Senior Minister: Will you now respond to this vow of dedication? We, the congregation of _____ Church assembled here do solemnly vow that we will support our ministers in the work they do for God.

People: We do.

Senior Minister: Do you now accept _____ as your associate minister, and pledge to give him your love, your friendship, and your full cooperation?

People: We do.

Senior Minister: The pronouncement

I now pronounce that you, _____, are duly installed as associate minister of the _____
Church, and may God richly bless our joint ministry.

Hymn of Fellowship: "Are Ye Able?"

Benediction: By the newly installed associate minister.

"The Lord bless thee, and keep thee: The Lord make his face to shine upon thee, and be gracious unto thee: The Lord lift up his countenance upon thee, and give thee peace" (Num. 6:24-26). Amen.

A fellowship hour or reception to follow

Installing the New Associate Minister

Service 3

Name of Church
Name of Denomination
City and State
A Service of Installation
for
Name of Associate Minister
Time and Date

Senior Minister Presiding

Prelude
Call to Worship:

"The Lord hath prepared his throne in the heavens; and his kingdom ruleth over all. Bless the Lord, ye his angels, that excel in strength, that do his commandments, hearkening unto the voice of his word.

Bless ye the Lord, all ye his hosts; ye ministers of his, that do his pleasure. Bless the Lord, all his works in all places of his dominion. Bless the Lord, O my soul'' (Ps. 103:19-22).

Hymn: ''Jesus Calls Us''

Invocation Prayer:

Our Father, we know that Jesus calls us to build thy kingdom on this earth. We would lay good foundations, and clasping hands in fellowship, work together to do thy will. Bless this day and be with us in this service. May we feel thy presence, and know thy love for us, that in turn we may truly love each other. This we ask in the name of thy Son Jesus. Amen.

Anthem or Special Music: ''Seek Ye the Lord''—Humphrey

Scripture Lesson: Luke 14:27-35

Pastoral Prayer:

Our Father, who art in heaven and on earth, who art in the hearts of men and in the greatness of the universe: Be with us and bless this hour the thoughts of our mind, the words of our lips, the work of our hearts and hands. We ask thy mercy and comfort for the sick, and on those who mourn in sadness—bless with thy presence those who are lonely. Let us this day begin to build on a strong foundation of the ministry and membership, the church that thou wouldst have us to build. May we, together, grow in grace and the knowledge of our Lord Jesus Christ. Help us to study thy holy Word, that our lives may be worthy. Keep us ever in thy care: correct us when we are wrong; bless us when we are right, and lead us ever onward toward thine eternal kingdom of love and light. All this we pray in the name of our redeemer, Jesus Christ. Amen.

The Message: How Firm a Foundation

(Notes which may be helpful)

This is the time for us, together, to lay a firm foundation.

With the help of the new associate minister we shall go forward with God's work.

We shall build in evangelism.

We shall build in Christian education.

We shall build in mission.

Together, with God's help, we will lay a firm foundation and build a strong church upon it.

Offering:

Hymn: "How Firm a Foundation"

Senior Minister: Will the new associate minister, _____ _____, and the congregation now stand and face each other to repeat solemn vows?

Associate Minister: I, _____, now solemnly vow to be a good minister to this congregation, and for God. I willingly accept this task, remembering always that I am a minister of God, and responsible for the preaching of his Word and the furthering of his work in this church and this community. I will be a helper to our senior minister, and try to uphold the work he attempts for God. With God's help I shall fulfill worthily the task for which I have been called.

Congregation: (In unison, reading from bulletin.)

We, the congregation of _____ Church solemnly covenant and pledge that we will accept _____ _____ as our associate minister, and that we will try to encourage and help the ministers in their task of promoting the kingdom of God. We will try to be helpful, not critical; building up, not tearing down the work. We promise to give of our time, our talents, and our money that God's will may be done in our church, in our community, and in our world. So help us God!

Senior Minister: Please remain standing for the pronouncement.

I do now declare that _____ is duly installed as associate minister of _____ Church, and may God add his blessing to this day.

Closing Hymn: "Softly and Tenderly Jesus Is Calling"

Senior Minister: Will our new associate minister now give the benediction?

Associate Minister:

"Now our Lord Jesus Christ himself, and God, even our Father, which hath loved us, and hath given us everlasting consolation and good hope through grace, Comfort your hearts, and stablish you in every good word and work" (2 Thess. 2:16-17). Amen.

A fellowship hour or reception may follow.

Ordaining/Installing Deacons (Elders, Stewards, etc.)

Service 1

Senior Minister Presiding: As part of our regular worship service

Minister: I have asked two of our serving deacons to assist me in this service of ordination/installation. (The two deacons join the minister.)

"And in those days, when the number of disciples was multiplied, there arose a murmuring of the Grecians against the Hebrews, because their widows were neglected in the daily ministration. Then the twelve called the multitude of the disciples unto them, and said, It is not reason that we should leave the word of God, and serve tables. Wherefore, brethren, look ye out among you seven men of honest report, full of the Holy Ghost and wisdom, whom we may appoint over this business. But we will give ourselves continually to prayer, and to the ministry of the word. And the saying pleased the whole multitude: and they chose Stephen, a man full of faith, and of the Holy Ghost, and Philip, and Prochorus, and Nicanor, and Timon, and Parmenas, and Nicolas, a proselyte of Antioch: Whom they set before the apostles: and when they had prayed, they laid their hands on them" (Acts 6:1-6). (Those churches who have elders may use Titus 1:5-9 in lieu of the above passage.)

Minister: Will those who are to be ordained/installed as deacons of the church please come forward and face the congregation?
(After they have come, to the congregation—) Are these the persons whom you have chosen to have spiritual care of this congregation?

Congregation: (In unison) They are!

Minister: Do you now hereby pledge yourselves to honor these deacons whom you have chosen, upholding them in their leadership and giving them your full cooperation in the upbuilding of Christ's church?

Congregation: (In unison) We do!

Minister: (To those deacons to be ordained/installed) Are you, who have been chosen in love by the will of this congregation, willing to undertake the station to which you have been called, and will you undertake the spiritual watchcare of this church?

Elders: We will.

Minister: The Scriptures tell us:

"Feed the flock of God which is among you, taking the oversight thereof, not by constraint, but willingly; not for filthy lucre, but of a ready mind; Neither as being lords over God's heritage, but being ensamples to the flock. And when the chief Shepherd shall appear, ye shall receive a crown of glory that fadeth not away. Likewise ye younger, submit yourselves unto the elder. Yea, all of you be subject one to another, and be clothed with humility: for God resisteth the proud, and giveth grace to the humble" (1 Pet. 5:2-5).

Minister: (To the deacons to be ordained/installed)
Our loving Heavenly Father, we come before thee and place these chosen servants before thee for thy blessing. We ask that they may be truly consecrated by thee, and that thou wilt lead them in the fulfillment of the duties they have accepted in thy church. May they be faithful servants of thine, and attend to the spiritual welfare of this congregation. We ask all this in Jesus' name. Amen.

Minister: Will the deacons now kneel for the laying on of hands? (As the deacons kneel, the minister places his hand on the head of one of the deacons, and the two assisting deacons place their hands upon his. As the service progresses, they move their hands till they have been placed on the head of each deacon to be ordained. The minister reads as they do this.)

Minister: Paul said:
"Till I come, give attendance to reading, to exhortation, to doctrine. Neglect not the gift that is in thee, which was given thee by prophecy, with the laying on of the hands of the presbytery" (1 Tim. 4:13-14).

Minister: Upon you rests the blessing of God, and the office of deacon in this congregation is hereby conferred upon you. May God grant you wisdom and love to serve the flock with diligence, patience, and affection.

May the Lord fill you with all spiritual grace, and make you truly a blessing to this congregation and a true servant of Almighty God. You are now duly ordained/installed as deacons. May God's richest blessings be yours. In Jesus' name. Amen.

Minister: You may now rise and return to your places.

At this point the regular worship service will resume.

Ordaining/Installing Deacons

Service 2

Senior Minister Presiding: As part of regular worship service

Minister: I have asked two of our deacons to assist me in this service of ordination/installation for new deacons. (The two deacons join the minister.)

"Likewise must the deacons be grave, not doubletongued, not given to much wine, not greedy of filthy lucre; Holding the mystery of the faith in a pure conscience. And let these also first be proved; then let them use the office of a deacon, being found blameless. Even so must their wives be grave, not slanderers, sober, faithful in all things. Let the deacons be the husbands of one wife, ruling their children and their own houses well. For they that have used the office of a deacon well purchase to themselves a good degree, and great boldness in the faith which is in Christ Jesus" (1 Tim. 3:8-13).

Hymn: "Take My Life, and Let It Be"

Minister: Will those to be ordained or installed as deacons of this church please come forward and face the congregation?

(To the congregation—)

Are these the persons whom you have chosen to have spiritual care of this congregation?

Congregation: They are!

Minister: Will you now vow and covenant that you will uphold these deacons whom you have chosen? Will you pray for them, honor them, and let them truly be your examples in following the way of Christ, our Redeemer? Will you be inspired by them, as they try in deep sincerity to live lives of purity and lead you in spiritual paths?

Congregation: We will.

Minister: (To the deacons to be ordained/installed)

After prayer and deep consideration, have you determined to undertake willingly the office of deacon in this congregation, and will you strive, to the best of your ability and with God's help, to lead the members of this church in spiritual growth? Will you comfort them in sorrow, counsel them in trouble, and visit them in sickness?

Elders: We will.

Minister:

"For they that have used the office of a deacon well purchase to themselves a good degree, and great boldness in the faith which is in Christ Jesus" (1 Tim. 3:13).

Minister: Will you now kneel to be ordained/installed? (The minister lays his hand on the head of one of the deacons to be ordained/installed, and the two assisting deacons place their hands on top of his. As he speaks, the minister moves their hands, till they have been laid on the heads of all those to be ordained/installed. Then other ordained persons will participate in the laying on of hands.)

Minister:

Dear Lord and Father, as we lay our hands on these deacons, chosen out of the congregation to be thy special representatives, wilt thou indeed consecrate them this day, that they may live lives of spiritual purity. Bless them, O God, as they try to be examples and leaders in this congregation. Grant unto them wisdom, understanding, and love, that we may truly honor them and support them. This we ask in the holy name of thy Son, Jesus. Amen.

Minister: You have now been duly ordained/installed as deacons of the church. Let your service in this office be a great blessing to this church, and may the congregation be ever glad that you have been chosen to serve as their leaders. God's richest blessings be upon the service of this day. In Jesus' name we ask it, Amen.

Minister: You may now rise and return to your places.

At this point the regular service of worship may resume.

Ordaining/Installing Deacons

Service 3

Senior Minister Presiding: As part of the regular worship service

Minister: I have asked two of our active deacons to assist me in this service of ordination/installation for deacons in our church. (The two deacons now join the minister.)

"And in those days, when the number of the disciples was multiplied, there arose a murmuring of the Grecians against the Hebrews, because their widows were neglected in the daily ministration. Then the twelve called the multitude of the disciples unto them, and said, It is not reason that we should leave the word of God and serve tables. Wherefore, brethren, look ye among you seven men of honest report, full of the Holy Ghost and wisdom, whom we may appoint over this business. But we will give ourselves continually to prayer, and to the ministry of the word. And the saying pleased the whole multitude: and they chose Stephen, a man full of faith and of the Holy Ghost, and Philip, and Prochorus, and Nicanor, and Timon, and Parmenas, and Nicolas, a proselyte of Antioch: Whom they set before the apostles: and when they had prayed, they laid their hands on them" (Acts 6:1-6).

Minister: Will those who are to be ordained/installed as deacons of the church come forward and face the congregation. (When they have assumed their places at front of church) Will all those who are presently members of the deacons please rise and stand in their places?

Minister: Will you, who are now members of the deacons, make welcome those who have been chosen to join you? Will you work with them in harmony and love, and so further the work of this church?

Deacons: We will.

Minister: Will the congregation now please stand?

Do you now affirm that these persons are chosen by you to become deacons in this church, and that you, the members of this congregation, will lend them every support as they attempt to carry out the many tasks assigned to their care? Do you vote to accept their service and give them loving support as needed for the upbuilding of the church?

Congregation: We do.

Minister: You may be seated. (Then speaking to those to be ordained/installed.) I now charge you that you be faithful servants of our Lord and Redeemer, Jesus Christ.

"But thou, O man of God, flee these things; and follow after righteousness, godliness, faith, love, patience, meekness. Fight the good fight of faith, lay hold on eternal life, whereunto thou art also called, and hast professed a good profession before many witnesses" (1 Tim. 6:11-12).

Minister: May we all be in prayer together, that these faithful persons may be ordained by God. Our merciful Father, we bring to thee these dedicated ones we have chosen to be deacons in thy church. Wilt thou indeed bless them, that they in turn may be a blessing to us all? May they serve thy children in all the tasks they are called to do. Help them to be dedicated servants, and give them wisdom and patience to serve well. This is our prayer this day, and we ask it in Jesus' name. Amen.

Minister: Will those deacons to be ordained/installed now kneel for the laying on of hands?

(The minister now places his hand on the head of one of the deacons to be ordained/installed, and the two assisting deacons place their hands on his. As the minister speaks, he moves his hand from the head of one deacon to another till his hand and the hands of the deacons have rested upon the head of each deacon to be ordained/installed.

Minister: Now may God's gracious benediction be upon you. We, by the laying on of hands, confer upon you the office of deacon, an honorable office, and one to be respected by every member of Christ's church. Now may our Lord fill you with zeal for the work, joy in the serving, and willingness to undertake great tasks in his service. You are now duly ordained/installed as deacons, and we commend you to the people. In the name of our Lord Jesus. Amen.

Minister: You may now rise and return to your places.

At this point the regular worship service will resume.

Ordaining/Installing Deacons

Service 4

Senior Minister Presiding: As part of the regular worship service

Minister: I have asked two of our active deacons to assist me in the service of the laying on of hands, by which we ordain/install our new deacons. (The two deacons join the minister.)

Minister:

"Grace be unto you, and peace, from God our Father, and from the Lord Jesus Christ. I thank my God upon every remembrance of you, Always in every prayer of mine for you all making request with joy, For your fellowship in the gospel from the first day until now; Being confident of this very thing, that he which hath begun a good work in you will perform it until the day of Jesus Christ: Even as it is meet for me to think this of you all, . . . inasmuch as both in my bonds, and in the defence of and confirmation of the gospel, ye all are partakers of my grace. For God is my record, how greatly I long after you all in the bowels of Jesus Christ. And this I pray, that your love may abound yet more and more in knowledge and in all judgment; That ye may approve things that are excellent; that ye may be sincere and without offence till the day of Christ; Being filled with the fruits of righteousness, which are by Jesus Christ, unto the glory and praise of God" (Phil. 1:2-11).

Minister: Will those to be ordained/installed as deacons please come forward and face the congregation, and will the congregation then rise also?

(When the deacons have faced the standing congregation, the minister continues.)

Minister: (To the congregation.)

Are these the persons you have chosen to honor with the position of deacon in the church?

Congregation: They are.

Minister: Do you now promise to accept them as your leaders, and help them in the tasks which they will do for the church? Will you cooperate and support them with your prayers and your work effort? For a deacon is a servant of the church, and as such will need your love and your help. Will you this day vow to be a help, not a hindrance, an encourager, not a critic, so that the work of the church may go forward and truly honor our Lord and Master Jesus Christ?

Congregation: We will.

Minister: (To the deacons to be ordained/installed.)

Will you this day pledge and affirm that you have accepted this office of deacon willingly and gladly, and that you will strive to the best of your ability, and with God's help, to fulfill all the duties involved in this office? Will you undergird your actions with prayer, and be responsible in carrying out those tasks assigned to you?

Deacons: We will.

Minister: Let us all bow together in prayer before we confer this office by the laying on of hands.

Almighty and everlasting God, nothing that we do here can be good unless thou art here to bless our words and our actions. Thou who ordainest all things, bless now this service, and consecrate to thy service these who here present themselves before thee. May thy grace be upon all, and may we together, have the fellowship of our Lord Jesus and the presence of thy Holy Spirit. This we ask in Jesus' name. Amen.

Minister: Will you now kneel together?

(The deacons to be ordained/installed kneel. The minister now lays his hand on the head of a deacon, and the two assisting deacons place their hands on his. The minister moves his hand to the head of each deacon, as he speaks, until the hands are laid on the head of each. Then all ordained persons present follow with the laying on of hands.)

Minister: Now our Lord God, as we lay our hands on the heads of these, thy servants, to ordain/install them as deacons of this church, wilt thou too ordain them, that they may be loyal workers, willingly accepting the tasks assigned to them and carrying them out with diligence and gladness.

Be thou their guide and ours, and help us together to worship and serve thee.

Let thy hand be upon us all this day, in Jesus' name. Amen.

Minister: I now declare that you are duly ordained/installed as deacons of this church. God bless you in all you do. You may now return to your places.

At this point the regular worship service will resume.

Dedication of New Communion Ware

Senior Minister Presiding: A complete morning worship service

Words of Reverence

Prelude
Call to Worship:

"This I say then, Walk in the Spirit, and ye shall not fulfill the lust of the flesh. But the fruit of the Spirit is love, joy, peace, longsuffering, gentleness, goodness, faith, Meekness, temperance: against such there is no law. And they that are Christ's have crucified the flesh with the affections and lusts. If we live in the Spirit, let us also walk in the Spirit" (Gal. 5:16,22-25).

Hymn of Praise: "Here, O My Lord, I See Thee Face to Face"
Invocation and the Lord's Prayer:

Eternal God and Father, we would invoke thy presence this day. Wilt thou be gracious and merciful to us, ready to forgive our sins and renew our relationship with thee? We pray that through following thy Son Jesus Christ, our Redeemer and Savior, we may come at last to the fullness of that abundant life which he has promised. Take thou our hearts and our lives and remold them as thou wouldst have them.

Teach us to mean every word as we pray the prayer that Jesus taught us, saying:

"Our Father which art in heaven, Hallowed be thy name. Thy kingdom come. Thy will be done in earth, as it is in heaven. Give us this day our daily bread. And forgive us our debts, as we forgive our debtors. And lead us not into temptation, but deliver us from evil: For thine is the kingdom, and the power, and the glory, for ever. Amen" (Matt. 6:9-13).

Scripture Reading: Luke 22:7-19
Anthem or Solo: "Communion Hymn"—Opie (or) "Send Out Thy Light"—Gounod

Words of Appreciation

Minister: We have met here this Lord's Day to celebrate with joy the dedication of our new communion ware.

We are aware that it is through the blessing and leading of God that we have been brought to this day. Hearts have been touched, so that we have received generous gifts that have made it possible for us to purchase these lovely emblems of service in our church.

(If the communion ware has been given as a memorial, then the minister may add—)

It is most fitting that this lovely service be a memorial to _____ _____ a devoted Christian, and one who has served God and the church well. It has been given through the generosity of _____ and we ask God's blessing upon the communion ware, those who have given it, and all of us as we bow before God.

Hymn: "Here at Thy Table Lord, This Sacred Hour"
Meditation Message: Behold, What Love!
(Notes which might be helpful in preparation)

Behold what love the Father has, that we should be called his children!

If we are all God's children, we must all love each other and serve one another.

Every time we partake of communion together, we must be reminded of the great love Jesus had for us, that he was willing even to go to the cross, and his death thereon.

But let it also remind us that he rose again—and walks with us. Let this be a day of consecration for each one of us.

Minister: Pastoral Prayer

Here, O Father, we bow in prayer before thee. We bring to thee our loved ones near and far. We would here remember and ask thy blessing on those of our members who are ill or housebound, and unable to be with us. Touch them with thy healing hand and may they know thy love, and be aware that we think of them and love them, too. Wilt thou forgive our sins, for we know that we have all sinned and fallen short of the glory of God. Restore us to wholeness and give peace within our souls. Do thou bless this day and make it a holy day of remembering for us. As we prepare for communion together, we ask that we may feel thy presence and know thy love. Let thy love so fill us that it will reach out to our brothers and sisters in the faith, that we may all be held in the warmth of thy love, and serve together to bring in thy kingdom, for this we pray in the name of our Savior, Jesus Christ. Amen.

Minister: (As preparation is made to receive the morning offering):

God gives to us all richly, as we have communion with him. By our gifts and offerings, we return just a little of what he has given us.

The Offering Is Received:

Minister:

"Love ye your enemies, and do good, and lend, hoping for nothing again; and your reward shall be great, and ye shall be children of the Highest: for he is kind unto the unthankful and to the evil. Be ye therefore merciful, as your Father also is merciful" (Luke 6:35-36).

Father, take this, our offering, and use it for the furtherance of thy work on earth is our prayer in Jesus' name. Amen.

Words of Institution

Minister: Will you now join with me in a litany of dedication?

Minister: To the glory of our God who has created so much beauty in our world: To the eternal glory of God and his service—

Congregation: We dedicate this communion ware.

Minister: That it may add to the dignity and spiritual growth of thy people—

Congregation: We dedicate this communion ware.

Minister: That we may never partake of this bread, representing our Savior's body, and the cup, representing his blood, in any manner other than pure reverence—

Congregation: We dedicate this communion ware.

Minister: That the beauty of this communion ware may continue to be used with joy by those who follow us in the church, and that in the years to come they may continue to glorify God—

Congregation: We dedicate this communion ware.

Minister: That our lives and hearts, as well as this lovely communion ware may be consecrated to his service and that in love we may worship together, remembering the love of Jesus that led him to die on a cross for our sake. To his glory and the greater love of God—

Congregation: We dedicate this communion ware.

Minister:

"Who shall separate us from the love of Christ? shall tribulation, or distress, or persecution, or famine, or nakedness, or peril, or sword?" (Rom. 8:35).

"Nay, in all these things we are more than conquerors through him that loved us. For I am persuaded that neither death, nor life, nor angels, nor principalities, nor powers, nor things present, nor things to come, Nor height, nor depth, nor any other creature shall be able to separate us from the love of God, which is in Christ Jesus our Lord" (vv. 37-39).

Minister:

"For I have received of the Lord that which also I delivered unto you, That the Lord Jesus the same night in which he was betrayed took bread: And when he had given thanks, he brake it, and said Take, eat: this is my body, which is broken for you: this do in remembrance of me. After the same manner also he took the cup, when he had supped, saying, This cup is the new testament in my blood: this do ye, as oft as ye drink it, in remembrance of me. For as often as ye eat this bread and drink this cup, ye do shew forth the Lord's death till he come" (1 Cor. 11:23-26).

The Organ Plays Softly as the People Receive Communion

Minister: (When all have been served)

"And are built upon the foundation of the apostles and prophets, Jesus Christ himself being the chief corner stone. In whom all the building fitly framed together groweth unto an holy temple in the Lord: In whom ye also are builded together for an habitation of God through the Spirit" (Eph. 2:20-22).

"For as the body is one, and hath many members, and all the members of that one body, being many, are one body: so also is Christ. For by one Spirit are we baptized into one body, whether we be Jews or Gentiles, whether we be bond or free; and have been all made to drink into one Spirit" (1 Cor. 12:12-13).

"Now ye are the body of Christ, and members in particular" (v. 27).

Closing Hymn: "Break Thou the Bread of Life"
Benediction:

"Be careful for nothing: but in every thing by prayer and supplication with thanksgiving let your requests be made known unto God. And the peace of God, which passeth all understanding, shall keep your hearts and minds through Christ Jesus. Amen" (Phil. 4:6-7).

Dedication of New Pulpit Furniture

Senior Minister Presiding: As part of morning worship service

Prelude
Hymn: "We Would Be Building"
Minister: It is fitting that we pause to dedicate and consecrate whatever is new to be used in the house of God. We come today with hearts full of gratitude to God that he has made it possible for us to purchase this lovely new pulpit furniture. We are thankful to those who have given so generously of their worldly goods so that this dream has become a reality in the life of our church. (If the furniture has been given by an individual or a family as a memorial to some

member of the church, at this point the minister will express thanks to the donors, and honor the one who is so memorialized.)

Minister: In 2 Chronicles we read:

"And at the king's commandment they made a chest, and set it without at the gate of the house of the Lord. And they made a proclamation through Judah and Jerusalem, to bring in to the Lord the collection that Moses the servant of God laid upon Israel in the wilderness. And all the princes and all the people rejoiced, and brought in, and cast into the chest, until they had made an end. Now it came to pass, that at what time the chest was brought unto the king's office by the hand of the Levites, and when they saw that there was much money, the king's scribe and the high priest's officer came and emptied the chest, and took it, and carried it to his place again. Thus they did day by day, and gathered money in abundance. And the king and Jehoiada gave it to such as did the work of the service of the house of the Lord, . . . and also such as wrought iron and brass to mend the house of the Lord" (24:8-12).

The Offering Is Received: (This may be the regular Sunday morning offering, or it may be a special offering to help with the cost of the new pulpit furniture.) As the offering is brought forward, the choir sings:

Choir: "We Give Thee But Thine Own"

Minister: Now hear the reading from the New Testament:

"According to the grace of God which is given unto me, as a wise masterbuilder, I have laid the foundation, and another buildeth thereon. But let every man take heed how he buildeth thereon. For other foundation can no man lay than that is laid, which is Jesus Christ. Now if any man build upon this foundation gold, silver, precious stones, wood, hay, stubble; Every man's work shall be made manifest: for the day shall declare it, because it shall be revealed by fire; and the fire shall try every man's work of what sort it is. If any man's work abide which he hath built thereon, he shall receive a reward. If any man's work shall be burned, he shall suffer loss: but he himself shall be saved; yet so as by fire. Know ye not that ye are the temple of God, and that the Spirit of God dwelleth in you? If any man defile the temple of God, him shall God destroy: for the temple of God is holy, which temple ye are" (1 Cor. 3:10-17).

Minister: Whatever we bring into God's house, we must pray that he will consecrate and dedicate, so that it may be of service to his house and to his people. Will you now join me in reading responsively?

Minister: "Blessed are the undefiled in the way, who walk in the law of the Lord.

Congregation: "Blessed are they that keep his testimonies, and that seek him with their whole heart. They also do no iniquity: they walk in his ways.

Minister: "Thou hast commanded us to keep thy precepts diligently.

Congregation: "O that my ways were directed to keep thy statutes! then shall I not be ashamed, when I have respect unto all thy commandments.

Minister: "I will praise thee with uprightness of heart, when I shall have learned thy righteous judgments. I will keep thy statutes: O forsake me not utterly.

Congregation: "Wherewithal shall a young man cleanse his way? by taking heed thereto according to thy word.

Minister: "With my whole heart have I sought thee: O let me not wander from thy commandments. Thy word have I hid in mine heart, that I might not sin against thee.

Congregation: "Blessed art thou, O Lord: teach me thy statutes.

Minister: "With my lips have I declared all the judgments of thy mouth. I have rejoiced in the ways of thy testimonies, as much as in all riches.

Congregation: "I will meditate in thy precepts, and have respect unto thy ways.

Minister: "I will delight myself in thy statutes: I will not forget thy word. Deal bountifully with thy servant, that I may live, and keep thy word.

Congregation: "Open thou mine eyes, that I may behold wondrous things out of thy law. I am a stranger in the earth: hide not thy commandments from me" (Ps. 119:1-19).

Minister: Now may we, as the people of God, here dedicate to his service this beautiful new pulpit furniture. May it always be used to his glory and in reverent service to him.

Will you now bow your heads for prayer with me?

Minister: Prayer of Dedication

Our kind and loving Father—yet art thou God of the universe! We bow humbly before thee this day, acknowledging that we have no power to bless, but seek thy blessing. We can in no sense consecrate, and so we ask that thou wilt accept this pulpit furniture and consecrate it to the purpose for which it was intended. Let everything we do in this church be done to thy glory and honor. May we, thy children, be welded together in love, so that we may be instruments, just as this pulpit is an instrument, to spread thy Word in a world that desperately needs it. Dedicate that which we present before thee, and consecrate our lives to thy service, for we ask this in the name of our Redeemer, Jesus Christ. Amen.

At this point the regular morning worship service will resume.

PART 2
AREA OF CHURCH MUSIC

As we approach the area of church music, perhaps the first thing that comes to mind is that beauty must indeed be an aspect of the very nature of God.

"When I consider thy heavens, the work of thy fingers, the moon and the stars, which thou hast ordained; What is man, that thou art mindful of him? and the son of man, that thou visitest him? For thou hast made him a little lower than the angels, and hast crowned him with glory and honour" (Ps. 8:3-5).

God has indeed made everything beautiful in its time. He makes flowers bloom in desert places where no one but he can see. Songbirds trill lovely melodies in the lonely woods and mountains, where no one listens but God, himself. Surely the God who painted the lovely dawns and sunsets is a God to whom beauty of sight and sound are very important!

It is most fitting that we give serious place to music in our church services, for it is so great a part of our worship of God.

The services in this section are again varied. There are long services prepared in such a way as to provide a complete worship service which may be mimeographed or printed in formal programs for the day.

The brief services are planned to be used at a chosen spot during the regular Sunday morning worship service, and incorporated into that service.

It is my hope that all the services in this book may be easily adapted to the needs of particular churches, whether urban or rural, large or small.

Installing the Church Organist or Pianist

Service 1

Name of Church
Name of Denomination
City and State
A Service of Installation
for

_____

As Organist/Pianist
Time and Date

Senior Minister Presiding: A complete service

God Gave Beauty

Prelude
Minister: Call to Worship

"Make a joyful noise unto the Lord, all the earth: make a loud noise, and rejoice, and sing praise.
Sing unto the Lord with the harp; with the harp, and the voice of a psalm.
With trumpets and sound of cornet make a joyful noise before the Lord, the King" (Ps. 98:4-6).

Hymn: "Praise Him, Praise Him"
Minister: Invocation Prayer

Almighty and Eternal God, thou art the God of creation, of order, and of beauty. We come before thee this day, asking that thou wilt bless us with thy presence in this special service in thy house. We thank thee that thou hast given us so much beauty in this world, and we ask that thou wilt help us to cherish that beauty, wherever thou hast placed it, and in whatever form we find it. Be thou here to bless and hallow what we do, and make us ever mindful of thy presence, for we ask it in the name of thy Son Jesus, our Lord. Amen.

Anthem or Solo: "If My People"—Owens
Scripture Reading: Psalm 150:1-6
Hymn: "God, Who Touchest Earth with Beauty"
Meditation: Let There Be Beauty—

(Notes that may be helpful)

God who said "Let there be light"—must also have said "Let there be beauty!" God has spoken in beauty in so many ways:

The beauty of a sunset, or a lake at dawn; a dew-touched flower, or a young girl in bridal gown.

If we seek beauty in life, we have little time to worry about ugliness.

God has spoken in music since the dawn of creation: the sighing of the wind (and man-made wind instruments); the chatter of a stream (and man-made cymbals and tambourines); the clear tone of the human singing voice (and man-made trumpets and horns).

Surely it is pleasing to God when we use all these instruments to enhance the beauty of the worship services in our sanctuary.

Pastoral Prayer:

Our loving Father, we bless thy name. May thy kingdom grow, and may we strive to do thy will at all times. Wilt thou bless those of our number who are ill and unable to join us on this joyous occasion. Do thou touch them with thy healing hand and help them to feel thy presence in their hours of need. Grant to us, thy children, those things that we need for our daily lives, and make us ever grateful for thy bounty. Be thou our guide and director, that we may keep to the path of the spiritual. Give us eyes to see the beauty in this world thou hast made, and give us ears to hear beautiful music and the voices of those that we love. May we praise and glorify thee in all that we do, and make us to follow in the pathway of our Savior, thy Son Jesus, to whom be honor and glory in all things. In his name, amen.

Offering Will Be Received

Offertory Prayer: We give thee but thine own, whatever the gift may be. We bring our tithes and offerings now before thee, and ask that what we give may be given from overflowing hearts, and that all may be used to further the work of thy kingdom. Bless our gifts, and bless us as we bow before thee. Amen.

Hymn: "Open My Eyes That I May See"

Minister: We are privileged to now install _____
_____ as our new organist/pianist. As a part of the formal service of installation, we have asked that he/she play a short organ/piano concert. May we prepare to listen with glad hearts.

Organ/Piano Recital

"Adagio Molto" from Third Organ Sonata—Alexandre Guilmant

"Now Thank We All Our God"—Siegfried Karg-Elert

"Panis Angelicus"—Cesar Franck

"Our Father Who Art in Heaven"—J. S. Bach

Minister: We are truly grateful for the beauty of the music we have listened to. In Isaiah we read, concerning the house of the Lord:

"The Lord was ready to save me: therefore we will sing my songs to the stringed instruments all the days of our life in the house of the Lord" (Isa. 38:20).

We are aware that they did not have organs or pianos in Bible days, but we know that many of the instruments they did have were used in the Temple services. Jesus attended those services, and surely he must have enjoyed the beauty of the music. At this time I would ask that _____ come forward and face the congregation. Will the congregation please rise?

Minister: (To the congregation)

Do you now accept _____ as our new organist/pianist? Will you give him/her your loyalty, allowing the music to help you with its beauty, and to undergird the reverence and dignity of our service?

Congregation: We do accept _____ as organist/pianist, and we will give him/her our loyalty.

Minister: (To the organist/pianist)

Do you, _____, now solemnly pledge that you will serve this congregation as organist/pianist? Will you strive to choose and play music that will enhance our worship by its beauty? Music is one of this world's beauties that we may offer to God, and will you try to remember always that we are offering this beauty at God's altar?

Organist/Pianist: I will.

Minister: I now declare that _____ is duly

installed as our organist/pianist, and I pray that ours will be a long and harmonious association. Together may we serve God, and help to guide man's thoughts to heavenly things.

(The organist/pianist returns to organ/piano.)

Hymn: "Lord, Speak to Me That I May Speak"

Minister: Benediction

"Speaking to yourselves in psalms and hymns and spiritual songs, singing and making melody in your heart to the Lord; Giving thanks always for all things unto God and the Father in the name of our Lord Jesus Christ" (Eph. 5:19-20).

The Lord be in your hearts always. In Jesus' name, amen.

A fellowship hour may follow

Installing the Church Organist/Pianist

Service 2

Senior Minister Presiding: As part of the regular worship service

Hymn of Preparation: "Living for Jesus"

Minister: We would pause in our worship service to install our new organist/pianist _____. Will he/she come forward please, and face the congregation as we join together in a responsive Scripture reading?

Minister: "Rejoice evermore. Pray without ceasing. In every thing give thanks: for this is the will of God in Christ Jesus concerning you" (1 Thess. 5:16-18).

Congregation: "Speaking to yourselves in psalms and hymns and spiritual songs, singing and making melody in your heart to the Lord" (Eph. 5:19).

Minister: "Giving thanks always for all things unto God and the Father in the name of our Lord Jesus Christ" (Eph. 5:20).

Congregation: We give thanks to God always for you all, making mention of you in our prayers (1 Thess. 1:2).

Minister: "Remembering without ceasing your work of faith, and labour of love, and patience of hope in our Lord Jesus Christ, in the sight of God, our Father" (1 Thess. 1:3).

Congregation: "Knowing, brethren beloved, your election of God" (1 Thess. 1:4).

Minister: "For our gospel came not unto you in word only, but also in power, and in the Holy Ghost, and in much assurance; as ye know what manner of men we were among you for your sake" (1 Thess. 1:5).

Congregation: "Let the word of Christ dwell in you richly in all wisdom; teaching and admonishing one another in psalms and hymns and spiritual songs, singing with grace in your hearts to the Lord" (Col. 3:16).

Minister: "And whatsoever ye do in word or deed, do all in the name of the Lord Jesus, giving thanks to God and the Father by him" (Col. 3:17).

Minister: Let us this day give thanks to God for this new relationship we are forging in the life of the church. May it be a rich blessing to us all, as we work together to glorify God through our worship, and through the beauty of church music.

Minister: (to the congregation)

Do you now promise to accept _____ as our new organist/pianist? Do you vow to give him/her your support, and honor the work we shall attempt together?

Congregation: We do.

Minister: (to the organist/pianist)

Do you, _____ , now undertake this task of being our church organist/pianist, and do you promise to lead us in the beauty of holiness?

Organist/Pianist: I do, with God's help.

Minister: I now declare that you are duly installed as organist/pianist of our church. May God add his blessing to this service.

(The organist/pianist returns to the instrument.)

Hymn: "I Would Be True"

At this point, the regular worship service will resume.

Installing the Church Choir Director (Minister of Music)

Name of Church
Name of Denomination
City and State
A Service of Installation
for

_____

as Choir Director
Time and Date

Senior Minister Presiding: A complete service of worship

Prelude
Minister: Call to Worship

"Make a joyful noise unto the Lord, all ye lands. Serve the Lord
with gladness: come before his presence with singing. Know ye that
the Lord he is God: it is he that hath made us, and not we ourselves;
we are his people, and the sheep of his pasture" (Ps. 100:1-3).

Hymn: "Wonderful Words of Life"
Minister: Invocation Prayer

Come into this place, our Father God, and bless us with thy loving
presence. Send down thy light and thy truth and let them lead us in
the paths of righteousness for thy name's sake. Teach us to so live
that we may follow our Lord, thy Son Jesus, and that he shall make
our lives a song of joy. Hallow this day and this service to thy
purposes, for we ask it in our Savior's name. Amen.

Anthem or Solo: "Because He Lives"—Gaither
Minister: Scripture Reading

"My heart is fixed, O God, my heart is fixed: I will sing and give
praise. Awake up, my glory; awake psaltery and harp: I myself will

awake early. I will praise thee, O Lord, among the people: I will sing unto thee among the nations. For thy mercy is great unto the heavens, and thy truth unto the clouds. Be thou exalted, O God, above the heavens; let thy glory be above all the earth'' (Ps. 57:7-11).

Solo: ''O Divine Redeemer''—Gounod
Meditation: Sing Praise
(Notes which may be helpful)

When we are glad, how can we help but sing praise to the Lord? God has given talents to each one of us, even if our talent is a cheering smile, an encouraging word to the despondent, or a charitable and loving act.

Even though talents are given us, they must then be cherished and developed. We must practice the pleasant smile, the cheering word, the charitable act.

We must continually remember to be encouraging, not critical. And we must foster within ourselves the love that expresses itself in the loving, charitable act.

If God has blessed us with a good voice, we should use it to His glory. Many use their talents solely for their personal profit, and this is wrong.

When one has musical talent and a lovely voice, it still takes study and effort and practice to develop that talent so that one may lead others.

Those who lead the music and direct the choir in our church have worked hard to attain their knowledge and proficiency. God is forever glorified through song and worship, and we should all sing praise to our God.

Minister: Pastoral Prayer and the Lord's Prayer

Our Heavenly Father, we would sing psalms and hymns and spiritual songs to thee, for our hearts overflow with gratitude and gladness. We know that thou art a God of beauty and gladness and melody. Enter thou into the hearts of thy people, that they may truly sing and be glad in thy holy temple. Touch with thy healing hand those of our number who are ill, and so unable to be with us on this glad day. Comfort the sorrowing; cheer the despondent. Help us all to develop those talents thou hast given us, that in all ways we may glorify thee, for we ask this all in the name of thy Son, who taught us to pray:

"Our Father which art in heaven, Hallowed be thy name. Thy kingdom come. Thy will be done in earth, as it is in heaven. Give us this day our daily bread. And forgive us our debts, as we forgive our debtors. And lead us not into temptation, but deliver us from evil: For thine is the kingdom, and the power, and the glory, for ever. Amen" (Matt. 6:9-13).

Offering to Be Received at This Point:
(As offering is brought forward, choir sings: "All Things Come of Thee, O Lord")

Minister: Will our new choir director _____
please come forward and face the congregation, and will the congregation please rise?

Minister: (To the congregation)
Do you, the congregation of _____ Church, solemnly vow that you accept _____ as choir director, and that you will support him/her in all efforts to glorify God through music and song?

Congregation: We do so vow.

Minister: (to the new choir director)

Do you, _____, likewise accept willingly the task of leading our choir? And do you promise, with them to lead our congregation in expressing their thankfulness to God in melody?

Choir Director: With God's help, I do.

Minister: I now pronounce you, _____, duly installed as our new choir director. May God add his blessing to the service you will render.

Minister: Will you all remain standing as we sing the doxology, and may God dismiss us with his blessing.

Unison: "Praise God, From Whom All Blessings Flow"

A fellowship hour may follow if desired.

Dedication of New Organ or Piano

Name of Church
Name of Denomination
City and State
A Service of Dedication
for
New Organ or Piano
Time and Date

Senior Minister Presiding: A complete worship service

Prelude

Minister: Call to Worship

"Let the word of Christ dwell in you richly in all wisdom; teaching and admonishing one another in psalms and hymns and spiritual songs, singing with grace in your hearts to the Lord. And whatsoever ye do in word or deed, do all in the name of the Lord Jesus, giving thanks to God and the Father by him" (Col. 3:16).

Hymn: "Praise Him, Praise Him"

Minister: Words of Greeting

We are met this day in a glad service of celebration. I am sure you are all aware what a wonderful addition to our worship of God is the new organ/piano recently installed. The sacrificial giving of many church members has made possible the purchase of this lovely organ/piano. We have all had our share in this, and we are thankful to God that he has made it possible to bring us to this day in the life of our church.*

(Alternative wording, if the organ/piano has been given as a memorial by some church family or friend.)

*We are deeply indebted to _____ for their generous gift of this organ/piano as a memorial to _____ _____. We share their love, and honor the memory of this dedicated Christian.

Minister: Invocation Prayer

Dear Heavenly Father, we now invoke thy presence. Wilt thou be here with us in our service, that we may truly worship thee, and that the dedication of this new instrument to thy glory may add beauty to our services, and so redound to thy adoration and reverence. For we ask that thou wilt share in this service, in the name of thy Son Jesus, our Lord. Amen.

Anthem: "The Worship of God in Nature"—Beethoven

Minister: Will you join in the responsive reading?

"O sing unto the Lord a new song: for he hath done marvellous things: his right hand, and his holy arm, hath gotten him the victory.

Congregation: "The Lord hath made known his salvation: his righteousness hath he openly shewed in the sight of the heathen.

Minister: "He hath remembered his mercy and his truth toward the house of Israel: all the ends of the earth have seen the salvation of our God.

Congregation: "Make a joyful noise unto the Lord, all the earth: make a loud noise, and rejoice, and sing praise.

Minister: "Sing unto the Lord with the harp; with the harp and the voice of a psalm.

Congregation: "With trumpets and sound of cornet make a joyful noise before the Lord, the King.

Minister: "Let the sea roar, and the fulness thereof; the world, and they that dwell therein.

Congregation: "Let the floods clap their hands: let the hills be joyful together before the Lord: for he cometh to judge the earth: with righteousness shall he judge the world, and the people with equity" (Ps. 98).

Minister: "Make a joyful noise unto the Lord, all ye lands.

Congregation: "Serve the Lord with gladness: come before his presence with singing.

Minister: "Know ye that the Lord he is God: it is he that hath made us, and not we ourselves; we are his people, and the sheep of his pasture.

Congregation: "Enter into his gates with thanksgiving, and into his courts with praise: be thankful unto him and bless his name.

Minister: "For the Lord is good; his mercy is everlasting, and his truth endureth to all generations" (Ps. 100).

Hymn: "This Is My Father's World"

Offering:

Offertory Prayer:

Our Father, we thank thee that thou hast arranged our world so that in some measure we may give back to thee from the great bounty thou hast given unto us. Give us generous hearts, that we may give in love, as thou hast so richly given unto us through love. Bless our tithes and offerings that they may serve to advance thy kingdom in our world, for we ask it in the name of our Savior, who loved us so much that he was willing to give his life for us. Amen.

The Message: God Speaks Through Music
(Notes which may be helpful)

God speaks to us in many ways. He speaks with a voice of thunder, as in Beethoven's anthem "The Worship of God in Nature." He speaks with the whisper of a breeze, as in Debussy's *Clair de lune*. But best of all is when he speaks in our hearts in a still, small voice. Then he assures us of his love and care, and we rest secure, safe in the hollow of his hand.

Minister: Pastoral Prayer

Eternal Father, great Creator God, we beg that thou wilt speak within our hearts as we bow before thee. Holy is thy name, and we praise and reverence thee in the beauty of thy sanctuary. We pray that we may truly do thy will on earth, as we strive to be worthy of thy love. Wilt thou grant to us those things which we truly need to make life here on earth rich and abundant. Place thy love especially around those of our members who are ill, or sorrowing, or in pain. Help us too, to surround them with our human love. Wilt thou now consecrate this organ/piano to the enhancement of our worship of thee. May we be grateful, not proud. May we feel appreciation, not arrogance. These things we ask in Jesus' name. Amen.

Hymn: "How Firm a Foundation"
Minister: Words of Dedication

Will you now repeat with me these words of dedication? To the greater glory of God, and his worship

Congregation: We dedicate this organ/piano.

Minister: To the inspiration of the people, and their participation through singing

Congregation: We dedicate this organ/piano.

Minister: To the beauty which this lovely instrument may lend to our worship services

Congregation: We dedicate this organ/piano.

Minister: I now declare that this new organ/piano has been truly consecrated for the greater glory of God in our worship. May God add his blessing to this dedication. Will you now stand for the benediction?

Minister: The grace of the Lord Jesus Christ, and the love of God, and the communion of the Holy Ghost, be with you all. Amen.

A fellowship hour may follow if desired.

Dedication of New Choir Robes

Senior Minister Presiding: As part of regular worship service

Minister: We would pause now in our service to formally dedicate the beautiful new choir robes that our choir is wearing this day. Will the choir please come to the front of the church and sing an anthem from the pulpit—so that we may all see the new robes.

Anthem: "How Great Thou Art"—Hine

Minister: Let us now read the Scripture responsively:

"Rejoice in the Lord, O ye righteous: for praise is comely for the upright.

Choir: "Praise the Lord with harp: sing unto him with the psaltery and an instrument of ten strings.

Congregation: "Sing unto him a new song; play skilfully with a loud noise.

Minister: "For the word of the Lord is right; and all his works are done in truth. He loveth righteousness and judgment: the earth is full of the goodness of the Lord.

Choir: "By the word of the Lord were the heavens made; and all the host of them by the breath of his mouth. He gathereth the waters of the sea together as an heap: he layeth up the depth in storehouses.

Congregation: "Let all the earth fear the Lord: let all the inhabitants of the world stand in awe of him. For he spake, and it was done; he commanded, and it stood fast.

Minister: "The Lord bringeth the counsel of the heathen to nought: he maketh the devices of the people of none effect.

Choir: "The counsel of the Lord standeth for ever, the thoughts of his heart to all generations.

Congregation: "Blessed is the nation whose God is the Lord; and the people whom he hath chosen for his own inheritance.

Minister: "The Lord looketh from heaven; he beholdeth all the sons of men.

From the place of his habitation he looketh upon all the inhabitants of the earth.

He fashioneth their hearts alike; he considereth all their works.

Choir: "There is no king saved by a multitude of an host: a mighty man is not delivered by much strength.

Congregation: "An horse is a vain thing for safety: neither shall he deliver any by his great strength.

Minister: "Behold, the eye of the Lord is upon them that fear him, upon them that hope for his mercy: to deliver their soul from death, and to keep them alive in famine.

Choir: "Our soul waiteth for the Lord: he is our help and our shield. For our heart shall rejoice in him, because we have trusted in his holy name.

Congregation: "Let thy mercy, O Lord, be upon us, according as we hope in thee" (Ps. 33).

Minister: *The Vows of Dedication*

Do you, our choir, now dedicate these robes to the glory of God? Will you wear them with joy, and sing praise to our God, leading the congregation in worship through music?

Choir: We do now dedicate these robes.

Minister: Do you now, the members of this congregation, accept these new choir robes as useful to add to the beauty of our service? Do you solemnly dedicate them to the worship of God?

Congregation: We do now so dedicate these robes.

Minister: Please bow with me for the prayer of dedication.

Dear Heavenly Father, we know that thou lovest beauty, because thou hast made our world so lovely. We thank thee that we are able to have these new choir robes, and so add to the dignity and beauty of our worship of thee. We cannot truly dedicate, but we come now humbly to thee, asking that thou wilt dedicate these new robes to the service of worship. We ask that they and we, thy children, may be acceptable in thy sight, and that thou wilt add thy blessing to this service of dedication. In Jesus' holy name we pray. Amen.

Hymn: "We Have Heard the Joyful Sound"

Minister: The choir may now return to its regular place, and we will continue with our worship service.

The Dedication of New Hymnals

Service 1

Name of Church
Name of Denomination
City and State
A Service of Dedication
for
New Hymnals
Time and Date

Senior Minister Presiding: A complete service

Prelude:

Minister: Call to Worship

"And the ransomed of the Lord shall return, and come to Zion with songs and everlasting joy upon their heads: they shall obtain joy and gladness, and sorrow and sighing shall flee away" (Isa. 35:10).

Hymn: "We Have Heard the Joyful Sound"

Minister: Invocation Prayer

Dear Lord, thou who wast near when we drew our first breath: Thou who hast guided us in dark days and in light, now be with us this day as we bow before thee. Wilt thou by thy presence, make this service holy in thy sight? As solemnly, yet joyously, we meet on this occasion, wilt thou fill us with thy Holy Spirit, that we may indeed say with Jacob, "Surely the Lord is in this place; and I knew it not" (Gen. 28:16). Bless all that we do and say here, that it may be acceptable in thy sight. In Jesus' name. Amen.

Minister: We do indeed feel great joy and gratitude to God that we have been able to purchase these fine new hymnals. We know that it is only by the grace of God, and the generous, sacrificial giving of many members of this congregation that we have come to this glad day of dedication.

or

These fine new hymnals have been made possible through the generous gift of _____, and they are given as a memorial to _____. We join together this day lovingly remembering this dear Christian and his/her great contribution to the life of the church. As we use these hymnals, we will be reminded always that his/her influence lives on in the hearts and lives of us all.

Minister: We have asked the choir to sing, as their anthem, one of the great hymns of the church.

Choir Anthem: "How Great Thou Art"—Hine

Minister: Scripture Reading—Psalm 95:1-7

The Message: Rejoice and Be Glad!
(Notes which may be helpful)

If we are truly Christian, we must be optimists.

If we truly trust God, we believe that all things work for good to those that love the Lord.

Jesus came to bring hope to a hopeless world: to teach love to a loveless world: to show mercy to a merciless world: and to show God to a godless world.

This is the world that the Lord has made. We will be glad and rejoice in it, with gladness and joy, singing praises to our Lord and King.

Minister: At this point in our dedication service, we would like to have a good old-fashioned hymn-sing.

Will you select your favorite hymns from our new hymnals, and call out the numbers, and we will sing the first and last verse of each hymn selected.

Hymns That May Be Used As Starters   (If members are slow to select):
   "Amazing Grace"
   "The Old Rugged Cross"
   "In the Garden"
   "I Will Sing the Wondrous Story"
   (Allow at least fifteen minutes of hymn-singing.)

Pastoral Prayer and the Lord's Prayer:

O Lord and Father of us all, thou hast taught us that our prayers to thee should be for ourselves, for our fellow Christians, and for those in authority over nations, and for all thy children in this vast universe. Be thou here in our midst, and hallow this day in our hearts. Place thy loving hand on those who are ill and in pain, and enable them to understand thy love and care. Bless with thy comfort those who sorrow this day. Guide the decisions of those in power in all the nations, and lead them in the paths of peace and brotherhood. Now bless us, as we wait before thee, and as we hold new hymnals in our hands, do thou consecrate them to thy service as only thou canst, for we ask all this in the name of our Lord Jesus.

And now will you repeat with the prayer he taught us, saying:

"Our Father, which art in heaven, Hallowed be thy name. Thy kingdom come. Thy will be done in earth, as it is in heaven. Give us this day our daily bread. And forgive us our debts, as we forgive our debtors. And lead us not into temptation, but deliver us from evil: For thine is the kingdom, and the power, and the glory for ever. Amen" (Matt. 6:9-13).

Minister: Will you all now join me in the litany of dedication? To the glory of God and the joy of singing praises to his holy name
Congregation: We now dedicate these hymnals.
Minister: That we may truly tell the wondrous story of Jesus' love, and how he came to earth to teach and to save mankind. So that we may gladly sing his praise
Congregation: We now dedicate these hymnals.
Minister: So that we will always remember the generous giving from loving hearts that made the purchase of these books possible
Congregation: We now dedicate these hymnals.

Minister: So that we will always use these hymnals with reverence, as something that belongs to God

Congregation: We hereby dedicate ourselves.

Minister: Will you bow with me for the dedicatory prayer?

Father, wilt thou consecrate and dedicate to thy service these hymnals, and the hymns and songs they contain. Help us to use them with joy, in praise to thee, and with our hearts and minds fixed on thee, for we ask it now in thy Son's name. Amen.

Hymn: "We Will Sing the Wondrous Story"

Minister: Benediction

"Now the God of hope fill you with all joy and peace in believing, that ye may abound in hope through the power of the Holy Ghost" (Rom. 15:13). Amen.

A fellowship hour may follow if desired.

Dedication of New Church Hymnals

Service 2

Senior Minister Presiding: As part of regular worship service

Hymn of Preparation: "Amazing Grace"

Minister: Please join me in a responsive call to worship, and a litany of dedication:

"O give thanks unto the Lord; call upon his name: make his deeds known among the people.

Congregation: "Sing unto him, sing psalms unto him: talk ye of all his wondrous works.

Minister: "Glory ye in his holy name: let the heart of them rejoice that seek the Lord.

Congregation: "Seek the Lord, and his strength: seek his face evermore.

Minister: "Remember his marvellous works that he hath done: his wonders, and the judgments of his mouth" (Ps. 105:1-5).

Words of Dedication

Minister: Unto thee, O God, eternal and glorious in the heavens, for the uses of service and worship

Congregation: We dedicate these hymnals.

Minister: For the encouragement of song in the hearts of our people. For the joy of our singing to the Lord

Congregation: We dedicate these hymnals.

Minister: To help us cultivate a love and appreciation of religious music. For the great hymns of the church, and anthems, and for fine gospel songs

Congregation: We dedicate these hymnals.

Minister: For the ministry of music to cheer our hearts and challenge our lives

Congregation: We dedicate these hymnals.

Minister: To lead us with music in the high, glad hours

Congregation: We dedicate these hymnals.

Minister: For the music to help us through our hours of pain, and trouble, and sorrow

Congregation: We dedicate these hymnals.

Minister: To help spread the good news of the gospel of Jesus Christ, through happy singing

Congregation: We dedicate these hymnals.

Minister: Will you now bow your heads with me for the dedication prayer?

Our dear Heavenly Father, we now ask that thou wilt accept these new hymnals, and consecrate them, in a way that we cannot—to thine own honor and glory. May we make them an aid in our worship, and may we use them always to thy greater honor. In the name of our Redeemer and Savior, Jesus Christ, we pray. Amen.

Hymn: "The Old Rugged Cross"

At this point the regular worship service will resume.

PART 3
AREA OF CHRISTIAN EDUCATION

Every area of work in the church is important. Surely the area of Christian education is pivotal, for it lays the groundwork for much of the church's work and mission.

Jesus was a Master Teacher, and it was spoken of him that he "taught them as one having authority, and not as the scribes" (Matt. 7:29).

Teaching is one of the fundamentals of the total life of the church. In large churches, it is possible to hire a director (or minister) of religious education who oversees the learning process throughout the church. We have included in this book installation services for the director of religious education who will be a staff member, directing the work of learning in the Sunday School, directing the youth program, and indeed being involved whenever the learning process takes place.

We realize that in the smaller churches, this grave responsibility falls on the volunteers who serve selflessly in positions as Sunday School superintendent, and those officers who serve with him/her. Therefore there are services included which will impress the importance of these positions, not only upon those who serve in that capacity, but also upon the congregation itself, as they see the officers formally installed.

Some doomsday prophets have commented that the church is in danger of dying out in every generation. If we neglect teaching and drawing into fellowship the youth and children, the church could die out with the elderly. Of course, that's not going to happen.

Teaching the Word is as important as preaching the Word. And we trust that these formal services of installation may help to emphasize this in the minds of all.

Installing the Director (Minister) of Christian Education

Service 1

Name of Church
Name of Denomination
City and State
A Service of Installation
for

_____

as Director of Christian
Education
Time and Date

Senior Minister Presiding: A complete service of worship

With All Thine Heart

Prelude
Minister: *Call to Worship*

"Come now, and let us reason together, saith the Lord: though your sins be as scarlet, they shall be as white as snow; though they be red like crimson, they shall be as wool" (Isa. 1:18).

Let us be truly in an attitude of prayer, laying our hearts, our souls, and our minds, with all our strength, before the Lord our God and asking that he truly consecrate us on this day. In Jesus' name. Amen.

Hymn: "Give Me Thy Heart"

Invocation and the Lord's Prayer

Minister: Our Father, which art in heaven and on earth, teach us to love thee with our whole hearts. Lead us in the paths of brotherhood and love with those with whom we share thy truth. We ask that thou wilt be with us, that the harmony and love we share in the church may be a challenge to those about us. Be thou near as we strive to grow in understanding of thy Word and thy way, and help us to worship in truth. May we together attempt to live thy way, as we pray the prayer Jesus taught us.

'Our Father which art in heaven, Hallowed be thy name. Thy kingdom come. Thy will be done in earth, as it is in heaven. Give us this day our daily bread. And forgive us our debts, as we forgive our debtors. And lead us not into temptation, but deliver us from evil: for thine is the kingdom, and the power, and the glory for ever. Amen'' (Matt. 6:9-13).

Anthem: ''My Tribute''—Crouch

With All Thy Soul

Hymn: ''Dear Lord and Father of Mankind''
Scripture Lesson:
Minister: 1 Corinthians 2:9-16
Message: All for Jesus
               (Notes which may be helpful)

Our Scripture lesson has told us how we are to love and to serve.

We are to worship with our hearts.

We seek communion with God, with our souls.

We study the Scripture to find our spiritual pathways, with our minds.

And we use every strength God has given us—mental, spiritual and physical—to follow in our Lord's way. ''And he answering said, Thou shalt love the Lord thy God with all thy heart, and with all thy soul, and with all thy strength, and with all thy mind: and thy neighbour as thyself'' (Luke 10:27).

Hymn: ''I Surrender All''
Offering:
Choir: ''We Give Thee But Thine Own''
               (As the offering is brought forward)

With All Thy Mind

Minister: We are most conscious of the importance of study in the life of the church. It is with this in mind that we have now called

_____ to be our director of Christian education.

It will be his/her task to oversee the total study programs of the church, to lead little children into a greater knowledge of the love of God, and to feel the love of our Savior, Jesus Christ.

It is a great and a holy task, and we have felt that we would install him/her in this worship service, so that we may all be truly aware of the seriousness and importance of the office he/she undertakes.

He/she will be in charge of our work with the youth of the church. This alone is a mighty task, for how precious to us all are the youth. There may be schools of prayer, of stewardship, of service, planned for the ongoing growth of the adults of the church. Indeed, _____ _____ will have much work to do.

The work of the church goes forward only as we undergird every effort with prayer, and I ask you to be much in prayer that our work may prove worthy in God's sight. Our minds are an important part of our being, just as our hearts and our souls are. We need to be challenged to think, and to study, and to grow.

Minister: Will you, _____ , now please come forward and face the congregation? Do you, _____ , now solemnly pledge that you will faithfully discharge the duties of director of Christian education in this church? Will you be often in prayer, and will you lead in study and spiritual growth both the children, youth, and adults so that they may all grow in understanding of God and his purpose for the church and for the world?

Director of Christian Education: I do solemnly swear that I will strive always to be worthy of the trust that you impose in me, and that I will try to continue to grow spiritually, that in turn I may lead others into the way of Christ. So help me God!

Minister: (To the congregation)
Will you please stand? Do you now accept _____ as director of Christian education in the _____ Church, and do you promise to give him/her your full cooperation? Will you pray for him/her, and to the best of your ability support the programs which he/she may initiate for the spiritual growth of our church?

Congregation: With God's help, we will.
Minister: *Prayer of Installation*

> Eternal and Almighty God, thou who hast given us heart, soul, strength, and mind with which to seek out thy truth and worship thee, we come before thee this day and ask that thou wilt indeed bless our total being. We would search for thee with everything that is within us. Grant to us the strength of purpose which holds steady and firm through all times, the days of joy and days of sadness. Bless now this service, that it may be pleasing in thy sight, and consecrate us that our total being may be dedicated to thee. Bless this, thy servant, who comes to us with deep desire to lead us in the paths of righteousness for thy name's sake. Help us to work together in harmony and affection, and give us thy blessing, for we ask it in the name of thy Son, our Teacher, Master, and Lord, Jesus Christ. Amen.

Minister: *Pronouncement of Installation*

> I now pronounce you, _____, duly installed as director of Christian education in the _____ _____ Church. May God bless you, and bless this association we have made, and may it serve to advance his kingdom, and upbuild his church. Amen.

Hymn: "Jesus Calls Us O'er the Tumult"
Minister: *Benediction*

> "Finally, brethren, whatsoever things are true, whatsoever things are honest, whatsoever things are just, whatsoever things are pure, whatsoever things are lovely, whatsoever things are of good report; if there be any virtue, and if there be any praise, think on these things" (Phil. 4:8).

> "And the peace of God, which passeth all understanding, shall keep your hearts and minds through Christ Jesus" (Phil. 4:7). For it is in his name we pray. Amen.

A fellowship hour may follow if desired.

Installing the Director of Christian Education

Service 2

Senior Minister Presiding: As part of regular worship service.

Minister: We would pause now in our service, to formally install _____ as our new director of Christian education. He/she has come to this day through a long period of study and dedicated loyalty to the church of Jesus Christ. We would recognize his/her dedication, and commend him/her to God, that he/she may be a blessing to us all, and lead us into higher pathways of study and understanding of the truths of God's Word.

Minister: Will _____ please come forward, stand before this congregation, and in the eyes of God prepare to take solemn vows?

Hymn: "Sitting At the Feet of Jesus"

(The new director of Christian education comes forward and takes his place before the congregation during the singing of the hymn.)

Minister: Truly, we would sit at the feet of Jesus, and study to deepen our understanding of his words and teaching. He was the great Master Teacher, and all of us who follow are led by his teachings.

Minister: Do you, _____, now solemnly vow that you will undertake the task as director of Christian education for the _____ Church, and that you will give it your prayerful, thoughtful, and loving service?

Director of Christian Education: I do so vow.

Minister: Will the congregation rise? Now do you, the members of _____ Church, vow that you will support the efforts of our new director of Christian education? Do you vow that you will study and be faithful to the teaching of our Lord Jesus, and uphold the hands of this, his servant?

Congregation: We do so vow.

Minister: I now pronounce you duly installed as our director of Christian education, and may God add his blessing to this service of installation.

Minister: *Prayer of Installation*

Dear heavenly Father, we have read in Proverbs the words: "Hear counsel, and receive instruction, that thou mayest be wise in thy latter end" (19:20). We would ask that thou wilt help us to take those words to heart, that we may truly grow in understanding and in the love for thy word. Bless this service, and bless this one who has come to serve with us. May he/she find truth and wisdom and ways to serve thee, for we ask it in thy Son's name. Amen.

At this point the regular worship service will resume.

Installing Sunday School Officers

Senior Minister Presiding: As part of regular worship service
Materials Needed and Instructions:
A vase on a small table at the front of the sanctuary.

Four file cards, on which are printed the responses for the officers. A branch of evergreen broken into four pieces, one piece to be given to each of the officers, with the file card appropriate to their office.

Minister: Today we have chosen to honor those dedicated Christians who have agreed to lead our Sunday School during the coming year. We want them to know that we appreciate their willingness to accept the task and their dedication to it. In the sight of God and this congregation, we would now formally install them. Will _____

_____, who has agreed to be the superintendent of the Sunday School, please come forward and stand before us?

Minister:

"The servant of the Lord must not strive; but be gentle unto all men, apt to teach, patient,

In meekness instructing those who oppose themselves; if God peradventure will give them repentence to the acknowledging of the truth" (2 Tim. 2:24-25).

As you place the small branch of evergreen in the vase, we would remind you that it is a symbol of **eternal life.** You will be leading

75

others in study. The example of your loyalty and faithfulness to duty will be a challenge to us all to grow in wisdom and understanding. We honor you for your willingness to serve, and we pledge you our support.

Sunday School Superintendent: (Reading from file card)

"Hear, O Israel; the Lord our God is one Lord: And thou shalt love the Lord thy God with all thine heart, and with all thy soul, and with all thy might. And these words which I command thee this day, shall be in thine heart" (Deut. 6:4-6).

I will strive to follow the teaching of our Lord Jesus and to be faithful to the task I have undertaken.

(He places his branch of evergreen in the vase and stands facing the congregation.)

Minister: Will _____ , the assistant superintendent of the Sunday School, come forward? You, _____ _____ , have agreed to be assistant superintendent of our Sunday School. You, too, hold evergreen. May it be a symbol to you of the **spiritual strength** which you will lend to our school. When the superintendent is absent, it will be your task to lead the Sunday School. At other times you will lend your help wherever it is needed.

"Train up a child in the way he should go: and when he is old, he will not depart from it" (Prov. 22:6).

In the Sunday School you will be dealing with children, our most precious gifts from God. May you lead well.

Assistant Superintendent:

"And Jesus increased in wisdom and stature, and in favour with God and man" (Luke 2:52).

I will try to be a help in the teaching process, and will be loyal to the task which I have undertaken.

(He places branch in vase and stands with superintendent.)

Minister: Will _____ , who is our new Sunday School Secretary, please come forward?

The evergreen which you hold in your hand represents **loyalty.** To you we entrust the keeping of records, and they are important. As you keep attendance records, you will be aware of members when absent, and together with the teachers, may seek to bring the absent back to their classes. In the Psalms we read:

"I will instruct thee and teach thee in the way which thou shalt go: I will guide thee with mine eye" (32:8).

May you follow God's guidance, always.

Sunday School Secretary:

"Blessed are they which do hunger and thirst after righteousness: for they shall be filled" (Matt. 5:6).

I will strive to follow God's guidance and be faithful to the task I have accepted.

(He places branch in vase and stands with other officers.)

Minister: Will _____, who is to be our Sunday School treasurer, please come forward?
The evergreen you hold in your hand represents *integrity and trust*. To you we entrust the physical need of our school.

"Both riches and honour come of thee, and thou reignest over all; and in thine hand is power and might; and in thine hand it is to make great, and to give strength to all" (1 Chron. 29:12).

Your task will be to deal carefully with offerings, keeping records, and expending for the needs of our Sunday School. God bless you for your faithfulness.

Sunday School Treasurer:

"Now therefore our God, we thank thee, and praise thy glorious name. But who am I, and what is my people, that we should be able to offer so willingly after this sort? for all things come of thee, and of thine own have we given thee" (1 Chron. 29:13-14).

(He places branch in vase, and takes his place with officers.)

At this time the regular worship service is resumed.

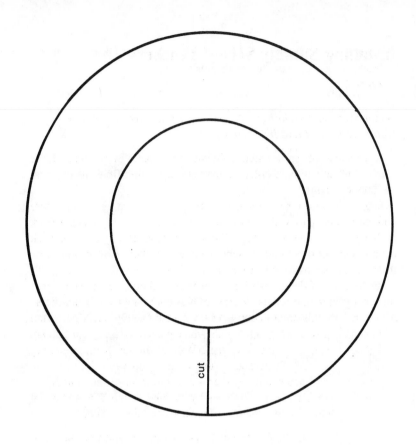

cut

Chart and Instructions:

Cut out construction paper "links" as shown below. Cut as many from each color as needed. Place piece of tape on one side, in order to fasten together.

Department	**Color**
Nursery	Red
Kindergarten	Blue
Primary	Yellow
Junior	Green
Middle or Junior High	Orange
High School	Tan
Adult	Lavender

Installing Sunday School Teachers

Service 1

Senior Minister Presiding: As part of regular worship service.
Materials Needed and Instructions:

A package of varicolored construction paper, from which large "links" for a chain are cut. Use the pattern for link from the chart on the previous page.

File cards, one for each teacher, on which are written the Scripture quotations and part which will be read by one teacher selected from each department in the Sunday School. Each teacher selected from each department in the Sunday School. Each teacher slips his/her link through another one, and fastens it with tape.

At the close of the installation service, there should be a large colored link chain extending across the front of the church, held by the teachers.

Minister: At this point in our service we would pause to recognize and honor those dedicated individuals who have agreed to be our Sunday School teachers for the next year. Will all the teachers, beginning with the Nursery Department, and working up from there, please come forward and stand together across the front of the church?

Minister: As a chain is made strong by its links, so our Sunday School is made strong by the quality of our teachers. Jesus said:

"I am the good shepherd, and know my sheep, and am known of mine. As the Father knoweth me, even so know I the Father: and I lay down my life for the sheep. And other sheep I have, which are not of this fold: them also I must bring, and they shall hear my voice, and there shall be one fold, and one shepherd" (John 10:14-16).

These are the shepherds of our flock, and we would honor them this day. I would ask each teacher to tell his/her name and the department where he/she serves.

(After each teacher has given his/her name, one speaks for the department, reading from the file card.)

Representative of Nursery Department:

"Then there were brought unto him little children, that he should put his hands on them, and pray: and the disciples rebuked them. But

79

Jesus said. "Suffer little children, and forbid them not, to come unto me: for of such is the kingdom of heaven. And he laid his hands on them, and departed thence" (Matt. 19:13-15).

We of the Nursery Department consider it a privilege to work with little children, and we ask God's help that we may teach well.

(The teachers from the Nursery Department fasten their links together, and stand at one side, holding the chain.)

Representative of (Preschool) Kindergarten Department (After the teachers have given their names):

"Verily I say unto you, Whosoever shall not receive the kingdom of God as a little child, he shall not enter therein. And he took them up in his arms, put his hands upon them and blessed them" (Mark 10:15-16).

We in the Kindergarten Department would receive each little child, remembering that we are all God's children, and that they, and we, need guidance along the pathway of life.

(The teachers of the Kindergarten Department fasten their links together and attach their chain to that of the Nursery Department)

Representative of (Younger Children's) Primary Department (After each teacher has given his/her name):

"Ye shall diligently keep the commandments of the Lord your God, and his testimonies and his statutes, which he hath commanded thee. And thou shalt do that which is right and good in the sight of the Lord: that it may be well with thee, and that thou mayest go in and possess the good land which the Lord sware unto thy fathers" (Deut. 6:17-18).

We in the Primary Department will try to help our students to do right and good in the sight of the Lord, that their lives, like the land in Bible times, may be worthy in the Lord's eyes.

(The teachers of the Primary Department fasten their links together, and join their chain to the Kindergarten Department chain.)

Representative of (Older Children's) Junior Department (After teachers have given their names):

"For whatsoever things were written aforetime were written for our learning, that we through patience and comfort of the scriptures

80

might have hope. Now the God of patience and consolation grant you to be likeminded one toward another according to Christ Jesus. That ye may with one mind and one mouth glorify God, even the Father of our Lord Jesus Christ'' (Rom. 15:4-6).

We would so lead the children who will be in our charge that they will say and do that which is right in the sight of God. To this aim, we pledge ourselves.

(The teachers from the Junior Department fasten their links together, and attach their chain to the Primary Department chain.)

Representative of the Middle, or Junior High (Younger/Youth), Department (After the teachers have given their names):

"These things command and teach.
Let no man despise thy youth; but be thou an example of the believers in word, in conversation, in charity, in spirit, in faith, in purity'' (1 Tim. 4:11-12).

We in the Junior High Department would truly become examples of good Christian behavior. We, the teachers, will strive to lead in the pathways of brotherhood, and peace, and patience, With God's help we will make this a good year in our department.

(The teachers of the Junior High Department fasten their links together, and then join their chain to the Junior Department chain.)

Representative of the High School (Older Youth) Department (After the teachers have given their names):

"And Jesus came and spake unto them, saying
All power is given unto me in heaven and in earth. Go ye therefore, and teach all nations, baptizing them in the name of the Father, and of the Son, and of the Holy Ghost.
Teaching them to observe all things whatsoever I have commanded you: and lo, I am with you alway, even unto the end of the world. Amen'' (Matt. 28:18-20).

We hope that in the year ahead we may lead our young people into ever higher paths of service to the church and to their fellowmen. We will try to be good teachers, and to serve the needs of the Sunday School, and of those young people entrusted to our care.

(The teachers fasten their links together, and attach their chain to that of the Junior High Department)

Representative of the Adults in Sunday School (After the teachers have given their names):

"For the Lord will not forsake his people for his great name's sake: because it hath pleased the Lord to make you his people. Moreover as for me, God forbid that I should sin against the Lord in ceasing to pray for you: but I will teach you the good and the right way. Only fear the Lord, and serve him in truth with all your heart; for consider how great things he hath done for you" (1 Sam. 12:22-24).

Indeed, the adults in our Sunday School classes and our teachers will be working together, and praying together, that they may grow in grace and understanding of our Lord's teaching. We ask that God will help us, for we need his help to understand and to teach. Amen.

(The teachers from the adult classes fasten their links together and attach their chain to the chain of the High School Department.)

Minister: As this colorful chain stretches across the front of our church, so the work of these teachers touches and helps us all. We ask God's blessing upon them as they begin this year, and we ask your prayers to undergird their work.

Minister: *The Pronouncement*

I now pronounce you duly installed as teachers in the Sunday School for the year ahead.

May God richly bless you and those you teach, is our prayer for you. In Jesus' name. Amen.

At this point the regular worship service will resume.

Installing Sunday School Class Officers

Materials Needed and Instructions:

A small table covered with a cloth should be placed at the front of the room. On it place a candleholder to hold a single tall, white candle.

Four file cards, on which are written the Scripture and statement each officer will use. These should be given the officers ahead of time.

One tall, white candle and matches

A Bible

A single flower in a bud vase

A small book of daily devotions or prayers

Installing Officer: We are met here to install the new officers of the _____ Sunday School Class. It is well that we do this, for it makes us all conscious of the responsibilities these officers have undertaken, and the enthusiastic support from each of us to which they are entitled.

"I beseech you therefore, brethren, by the mercies of God, that ye present your bodies a living sacrifice, holy, acceptable unto God, which is your reasonable service. And be not conformed to this world: but be ye transformed by the renewing of your mind, that ye may prove what is that good, and acceptable, and perfect will of God" (Rom. 12:1-2).

Installing Officer: Will _____ , the new president of the _____ Class, please come forward?

President (Places tall, white candle in holder and lights it.):

As your new president, I would say to you that this candle represents our Lord Jesus Christ, who said to us:

"Ye are the light of the world. A city that is set on an hill cannot be hid. Neither do men light a candle, and put it under a bushel, but on a candlestick; and it giveth light unto all that are in the house. Let your light so shine before men, that they may see your good works, and glorify your Father which is in heaven" (Matt. 5:14-16).

Installing Officer: Will _____ , your new vice president, please come forward?

Vice President: (Places open Bible on the table in front of the tall, white candle.)

As your vice president, I will assist the president in any way that I am able. This open Bible is to remind you that we must study and search the Scriptures, if we are to be truly Christian and follow the way of our Master, Jesus. Long ago the psalmist said:

"Blessed is the man that walketh not in the counsel of the ungodly, nor standeth in the way of sinners, nor sitteth in the seat of the scornful. But his delight is in the law of the Lord; and in his law doth he meditate day and night.

And he shall be like a tree planted by the rivers of water, that bringeth forth his fruit in his season; his leaf also shall not wither; and whatsoever he doeth shall prosper" (Ps. 1:1-3).

Installing Officer: Will _____, who is to be our treasurer, please come forward?

Treasurer (Places single flower in bud vase to left of Bible):

It will be for me to handle the things of this world, and I promise to handle them with care and integrity. God has made everything beautiful in its time. This flower represents the beauty of the gifts God has given us.

"Honour and majesty are before him: strength and beauty are in his sanctuary. Give unto the Lord, O ye kindreds of the people. . . . Give unto the Lord the glory due unto his name: Bring an offering and come into his courts. O worship the Lord in the beauty of holiness: fear before him, all the earth" (Ps. 96:6-9).

Installing Officer: Will _____, the new class secretary, please come forward?

Secretary (Places small book of devotions or prayers open and standing, at the right of the Bible.):

As your new secretary, I would remind you that constant prayer and daily devotions are important to the lives of us all. Only in this way can we grow as Christians.

"Now we exhort you, brethren, warn them that are unruly, comfort the feebleminded, support the weak, be patient toward all men. See that none render evil for evil unto any man; but ever follow that which is good, both among yourselves, and to all men. Rejoice evermore. Pray without ceasing. In everything give thanks; for this is the will of God in Christ Jesus concerning you" (1 Thess. 5:14-18).

Installing Officer: Now I declare that the officers of the _____ _____ Class of the Sunday School are duly installed. Will you all stand with me and join hands, forming a circle, the symbol of immortality, as we sing one verse of the closing hymn.

Hymn: "Blest Be the Tie That Binds"

PART 4
AREA OF CHRISTIAN
FELLOWSHIP

Fellowship is an important word in the church, and an important aspect of any Christian church. Without fellowship a church would be barren, indeed. In the church we have many fellowships. Every group that meets together is in truth a fellowship of saints. And Jesus said: "For where two or three are gathered together in my name, there am I in the midst of them" (Matt. 18:20).

In this section we have included long services that may be used as a program in itself, at a luncheon meeting or other special occasion. There are also briefer services which may be used at a meeting where there is a guest speaker or other special planned program.

Any one of these installation services will lend importance to the offices to which the members have been elected or appointed. They will impress upon those officers the solemn duties they have accepted, and the need for prayer and God's guidance as they fulfill those duties. Installing the officers formally will also impress upon the membership their need to support those officers to the utmost of their abilities.

The formal installation might be made by the pastor of the church, a former president of the organization, or a guest invited especially for the occasion. These services may require visual charts and instructions for their use. If charts are used, they will be placed before the installation service itself begins.

The titles for officers may be different in your organization. You may have other officers, or you may not have some of the officers included in these programs. They may easily be adapted by changing the title in each response. If your organization has fewer officers to be installed, just leave out the ones not needed.

We trust that these services may be used many times and prove useful to all those involved.

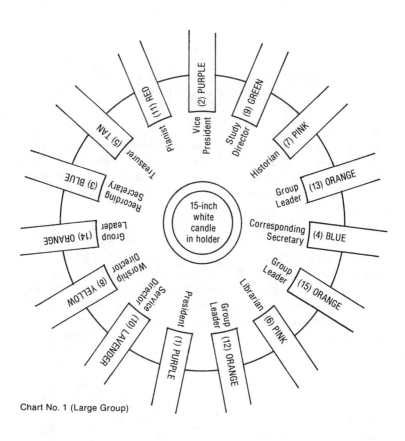

Chart No. 1 (Large Group)

86

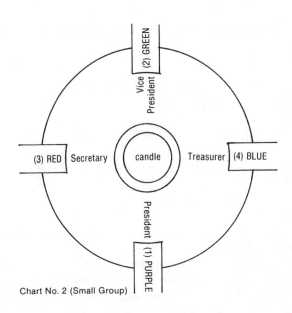

Chart No. 2 (Small Group)

Chart No. 3 (Be sure to place bottom row first, and work up.)

1	2	3	4	5
P	P	B	B	T
U	U	L	L	A
R	R	U	U	N
P	P	E	E	
L	L			
E	E			

6	7	8	9	10
P	P	Y	G	L
I	I	E	R	A
N	N	L	E	V
K	K	L	E	E
		O	N	N
		W		D
				E
				R

11	12	13	14	15
R	O	O	O	O
E	R	R	R	R
D	A	A	A	A
	N	N	N	N
	G	G	G	G
	E	E	E	E

Installing Officers of Women's Organizations

Service 1

The Wheel of Color

Materials Needed and Instructions for Use.

A small table

A white tablecloth

A 15-inch white candle in holder

A flat circle of Styrofoam (12 to 15 inches, depending on the size of the table.)

A roll of half-inch masking tape

A box of thumbtacks

15 lengths of one-inch satin ribbon, 12 inches long, in the colors suggested for the wheel.

(If it is difficult to buy Styrofoam, then make a simple white pincushion with a hole in center for the candleholder, marking the numbers on it. Or cut two circles from white poster board and glue them together, so that thumbtacks will stick in place.)

1 piece of white poster board, cut to a size so that the ribbons may be placed on it.

File cards for each officer to be installed with the words they will say typed or printed upon them.

Place small table in front of rostrum from which the installing official will officiate. Be sure that there is room to walk around the table. Place the white cloth on it, with the white candle in a low holder in the center. Cut a hole in the Styrofoam (or poster board or pincushion) so that it fits over the low candleholder.

Place small pieces of masking tape near the edge of the circle, as shown on chart No. 1, and mark with the numbers that you will be using.

For a large organization use chart No. 1. For a small organization use chart No. 2.

Place a small piece of masking tape on the end of each thumbtack, print the numbers on the tape, then match the tacks to the number and color of the officers to be installed. Place the thumbtack in the end of the colored ribbon. Allow a little masking tape to help hold the thumbtack in Styrofoam or card.

Using the thumbtacks, place the ribbons on the card chart No. 3. Place the bottom row first, then the middle row, and then the top, so the ribbons may be removed in regular order, 1-2-3.

To the Installing Officer:

As you read the name and title of office to which each has been elected, ask each individual to come forward. They will take from the card which you will hold the ribbon with a numbered thumbtack which represents the office they are to hold.

When all officers to be installed have been named and have been given their ribbon and the file card on which is written their vow, you are ready to proceed. It would be most helpful if at least one rehearsal were planned, so that the women can be familiar with the procedure.

Installing Official: (Lighting tall, white candle at center of the table, then returning to the rostrum)

Jesus said, "I am the light of the world: he that followeth me shall not walk in darkness, but shall have the light of life" (John 8:12). The tall, white candle in our worship center represents Christ, the Light of the World. He is our Master, and we follow him, attempting to live in the Christian way. You have been chosen to lead the _____ _____ organization for the next year. I challenge you to be worthy leaders, and to follow our Master and try to walk in his footsteps. I ask you now to form your wheel of color surrounding the candle which represents Christ.

President: No. 1 Purple (Holding her ribbon up for all to see. Each person who follows her, following the sequence of numbers on their ribbons, does likewise.) Purple is a royal color, and represents the authority and responsibility which I have undertaken in becoming your president.

(She places the thumbtack firmly in Styrofoam [using the tape to hold it secure] careful to match her number 1 to the number 1 in the Styrofoam circle. Each person will be careful to match their number with that in the circle.)

Jesus also said: "Ye are the light of the world. A city that is set on a hill cannot be hid. Neither do men light a candle and put it under a bushel, but on a candlestick; and it giveth light unto all that are in the house" (Matt. 5:14-15). I will try to let the light of Christ shine through me, that I may lead you well.

(She moves to one side and stands facing the people.

Vice President: No. 2 Purple   I, too, have a purple ribbon, as it shall be my task to stand beside your president, presiding in her absence, and strengthening her when we are together. (She places her ribbon in circle.) Jesus continued: "Let your light so shine before men that they may see your good works, and glorify your Father which is in heaven" (Matt. 5:16). This we, as your leaders, will strive to do. (She takes her place beside the president.)

Recording Secretary: No. 3 Blue   My ribbon is blue, representing faithfulness. I shall try to be faithful in all ways to the duties of the office to which I have been elected.

In the Book of Proverbs, we read: "When a man's ways please the Lord, he maketh even his enemies to be at peace with him" (16:7).

And again, "A man's heart deviseth his way: but the Lord directeth his steps" (Prov. 16:9)

We trust that the Lord will direct our paths in the year ahead.

(She takes her place beside other officers.)

Corresponding Secretary: No. 4 Blue   I too have a blue ribbon, and I vow that I will faithfully perform my duties as corresponding secretary. In the Book of Acts we read: "But the Lord said unto him, Go thy way: for he is a chosen vessel unto me, to bear my name before the Gentiles, and kings, and the children of Israel" (9:15).

We pray that we, your officers, may be instruments in the hands of God.

(She takes her place with other officers.)

Treasurer: No. 5 Tan   I hold in my hand a ribbon of tan, and to me this represents honesty and integrity, and attendance to the smallest detail. These are the qualities I hope to bring to my office as treasurer. The psalmist tells us:

"Lord, who shall abide in thy tabernacle? who shall dwell in thy holy hill? He that walketh uprightly, and worketh righteousness, and speaketh the truth in his heart" (15:1-2). And in 2 Corinthians we read: Providing for honest things, not only in the sight of the Lord, but also in the sight of men" (8:21). This will be my aim, this year.

(She takes her place with other officers.)

Librarian: No. 6 Pink   My pink ribbon represents the effort it will take, not only to keep up with my own worthwhile reading, but to support and lead us all into broader fields, by our reading. In the Book of John we find these words, "And there are also many other things which Jesus did, the which, if they should be written every one, I suppose that even the world itself could not contain the books that should be written. Amen" (21:25).

But there are in our world many books which can help us to learn more about our Lord and his ways. I vow to help us to find them.

(She takes her place with the other officers.)

Historian: No. 7 Pink   My ribbon too is pink. This reminds me that it is important to remember and save the good things of the past, and to look forward to the future with vision. Habakkuk tells us: "And the Lord answered me and said, Write the vision, and make it plain upon tables, that he may run that readeth it. For the vision is yet for an appointed time, but at the end it shall speak, and not lie: though it tarry, wait for it; because it will surely come, it will not tarry" (2:2-3).

So I ask you to wait with me, remembering the past, but looking to the future.

(She takes her place with the other officers.)

Worship Director: No. 8 Yellow   Yellow represents the light and joy of true worship. I vow that this year I will truly strive to lead in worship, setting aside time for prayer and quiet meditation on the things of the Spirit, so that we may all grow closer to God. In the Gospel of John we read: "God is a Spirit: and they that worship him must worship him in spirit and in truth" (4:24).

May we learn, together, to worship God "in spirit and in truth."

(She takes her place with the other officers.)

Study Director: No. 9 Green   My ribbon is green, and to me it represents life at its most abundant, and growing edge. To grow, we must study and have a true hunger for God and his way. In Psalm 143 we read: "I remember the days of old; I meditate on all thy works; I muse on the work of thy hands. I stretch forth my hands unto thee: my soul thirsteth after thee, as a thirsty land. Selah" (vv. 5-6).

Together, our souls will thirst for knowledge of the Lord, and through study we will grow in that knowledge.

(She takes her place with the other officers.)

Service Director: No. 10 Lavender   My lavender ribbon reminds me that my office as service director is to lead you in action. It is our task to be charitable, hospitable, and loving. Together we will undertake many tasks, and together we will work in the light of Christ. Jesus told us:

"And why call ye me Lord, Lord, and do not the things which I say? Whosoever cometh to me, and heareth my sayings, and doeth them, I will shew you to whom he is like: He is like a man which built a house, and digged deep, and laid the foundation on a rock: and when the flood arose, the stream beat vehemently upon the house, and could not shake it: for it was founded upon a rock" (Luke 6:46-48).

May we together, build well this year.

(She takes her place with other officers.)

Pianist: No. 11 Red   My ribbon is red, and well represents the cheerfulness added to our organization by music and singing. I vow to be faithful, and to give what talent I have, that we may all share in the joy of music.

Paul's Letter to the Colossians says: "Let the word of Christ dwell in you richly in all wisdom; teaching and admonishing one another in psalms and hymns and spiritual songs, singing with grace in your hearts to the Lord (3:16).

May we remember those words in the year ahead.

(She takes her place with the other officers.)

Group Leaders

Group Leader No. 1: No. 12 Orange   As group leaders, our ribbons are orange. I feel a great responsibility for the office which I have accepted. In the Book of Psalms we read: "Thou wilt shew me the path of life: in thy presence is fulness of joy; at thy right hand there are pleasures for evermore" (16:11).

May we together, experience that joy this year.

(She takes her place with other officers.)

Group Leader No. 2: No. 13 Orange   We hope to lead well and worthily in the sight of our Master, Jesus, for he said: "To him the porter openeth; and the sheep hear his voice; and he calleth his own sheep by name, and leadeth them out. And when he putteth forth his own sheep, he goeth before them, and the sheep follow him: for they know his voice'' (John 10:3-4).

May we, too, know his voice and follow him.

(She takes her place with other officers.)

Group Leader No. 3: No. 14 Orange   The orange color of my ribbon makes me remember that you thought me worthy of leadership. I shall endeavor to lead well, and make you glad you chose me. In the Ephesian letter we read: ''Be ye therefore followers of God, as dear children; And walk in love, as Christ also hath loved us, and hath given himself for an offering and a sacrifice to God for a sweet-smelling savour'' (5:1-2).

May we all truly walk in love through this year.

(She takes her place with other officers.)

Group Leader No. 4: No. 15 Orange   My orange ribbon reminds me of the way we began our wheel of color. John wrote: ''Then spake Jesus again unto them, saying, I am the light of the world: he that followeth me shall not walk in darkness, but shall have the light of life'' (8:12).

We have that light, and we vow to walk in it this year.

Installing Official: We have now completed our wheel of color, and I challenge you all to fulfill the vows you have made. Will the membership please rise, and repeat after me—We the members of _____, pledge that we will support these, our officers in the tasks they have undertaken, and that we will strive to be good followers, so help us God!

Installing Official: I now pronounce that your officers are duly installed.

Benediction

''Now God himself and our Father, and our Lord Jesus Christ, direct our way unto you. And the Lord make you to increase and abound in love one toward another, and toward all men, even as we do toward you: To the end that he may stablish your hearts unblameable in holiness before God, even our Father, at the coming of our Lord Jesus Christ with all his saints'' (1 Thess. 3:11-13).

Installing Officers of Women's Organizations

Service 2

Materials Needed and Instructions:
A small table with a white cloth.
An empty vase at the back of the table.
A Bible open to Galatians 3:28—propped up a little.
A flower of different color for each officer to be installed. (If a variety of colors of fresh flowers are available, they can be used. If not, artificial flowers may be substituted.)
Give each officer a file card with their response printed upon it, and a flower of the appropriate color.

Officer	Flower
President	blue
Vice President	yellow
Secretary	orange
Treasurer	red
Study Director	pink
Worship Director	white
Service Director	maroon
Group Leaders	salmon

All Children of God—Through Christ

Hymn: "In Christ There Is No East or West"

Outgoing President: (Expresses thanks for the year past, and introduces the installing official.)

Installing Official:

It is most fitting that we meet here this day to install the officers of the _____. These dedicated members have accepted the solemn responsibility involved in the offices to which they have been elected. The offices are an honor to those chosen to fill them, but also bring with them obligations and duties. We are all children of God through Christ, and we read in 1 John:

"Beloved, now are we the sons of God, and it doth not yet appear what we shall be: but we know that, when he shall appear, we shall be like him; for we shall see him as he is'' (1 John 3:2).

I consider it a privilege that you have asked me to install this slate of officers, and I ask that each officer will come forward as I call her name, and add her flower to our bouquet.

Installing Official: Will _____, your new president, come forward please?

President: (Places her blue flower in the vase.)

The color blue represents faith and loyalty, and I vow that I will be true to the office to which you have elected me. Flowers, like people, come in different colors, yet they are all part of the beauty God placed in the world. We, having differing talents and abilities, all serve God in our own way, as it is written:

"Now there are diversities of gifts, but the same Spirit. And there are differences of administrations, but the same Lord. And there are diversities of operations, but it is the same God which worketh in all" (1 Cor. 12:4-6).

With God's help I will serve as your president, and attempt to lead us all into a closer walk with him. As church women we must study to stretch our minds; worship to enlarge our souls; and we must reach out to others, and so widen our hearts.

I pledge you that I will be a faithful servant of our Lord Jesus Christ, as we work together to help build the kingdom of God.

Installing Official: Will _____, your new vice president, please come forward?

Vice President: (Places yellow flower in vase.)

Yellow is the color of sunshine, and represents cheerfulness. I will cheerfully support our president in those tasks that she undertakes, and I will try always to encourage more effort in charitable love, more creativity in our thinking, and a closer fellowship in our relationships with each other. The Scripture that _____ _____ read, continues:

"But the manifestation of the Spirit is given to every man to profit withal.

For to one is given by the Spirit the word of wisdom; to another the word of knowledge by the same Spirit;

To another faith by the same Spirit; to another the gifts of healing by the same Spirit" (1 Cor. 12:7-9).

So I would say to you all, that whatever gifts we have, let us use them in the work of our Lord Jesus. I pledge to you that I will strive to use whatever talent I may have to further his cause.

Installing Official: Will _____ , your new secretary, please come forward?

Secretary: (Places orange flower in vase)

Now we begin to see the variety of color in our flowers. They represent to us the variety of people, of all nations and colors, who are God's children, and make up his kingdom. Continuing again from the same Scripture, we read:

"To another the working of miracles; to another prophecy; to another the discerning of spirits; to another divers kinds of tongues; to another the interpretation of tongues: But all these worketh that one and the selfsame Spirit, dividing to every man severally as he will. For as the body is one, and hath many members, and all the members of that one body, being many, are one body: so also is Christ" (1 Cor. 12:10-12).

So we are one body. Although we are scattered over all the world, we are all his children. Sometimes we are stubborn children, seeking our own way. I promise that I will try to be his obedient child, seeking to perform the duties of my office as secretary in a way that shall be pleasing to him.

Installing Official: Will _____, your new treasurer, please come forward?

Treasurer: (Places red flower in vase)

My red flower represents the good earth. As your treasurer it will be my task to handle with honesty, integrity, and generosity the offerings we receive. It will be my duty to keep records, to draw checks when needed, and always to remember that a church organization exists to give, not to hoard its assets. The Scripture we have been reading now adds:

"For by one Spirit are we all baptized into one body, whether we be Jews or Gentiles, whether we be bond or free; and have been all made to drink of the one Spirit.

For the body is not one member, but many" (1 Cor. 12:13-14).

Truly we are one body, and members one of another. May we always be aware of this as we work together in harmony and love.
(She takes her place with other officers.)

Installing Official: Will _____, your new study director, please come forward?

Study Director: (Places pink flower in vase)
As your study director, I feel that my task is a solemn and important one. Together we shall be studying the Bible, seeking new light from God's Word, so that we may find God's will for our lives. Jesus "went about all Galilee, teaching in their synagogues, and preaching the gospel of the kingdom, and healing all manner of sickness and all manner of disease among the people" (Matt. 4:23).

Our Lord was a healer and a preacher, but he was also a teacher. May we together study to be better Christians in the year ahead.
(She takes her place with the other officers.)

Installing Official: Will _____, your new worship director, please come forward?

Worship Director: (Places white flower in vase)
White is the symbol for purity, and so my white flower signifies purity in worship.
As your worship director, I hope to lead you on ever deeper paths of worship and fellowship with our Lord Jesus Christ. So I pray,

"That Christ may dwell in your hearts by faith; that ye, being rooted and grounded in love,
May be able to comprehend with all saints what is the breadth, and length, and depth, and height;
And to know the love of Christ, which passeth knowledge, that ye might be filled with all the fulness of God" (Eph. 3:17-19).

May our search for God's will be rewarded by the sweetness of communion with our Lord Jesus, and may we together experience the fulness of God.
(She takes her place with the other officers.)

Installing Official: Will _____, your new service director, please come forward?

Service Director: (Places maroon flower in vase)

I add my flower to the arrangement in the vase, and perhaps we can begin to see the beauty that God sees. He has made flowers of all colors, and when placed together they make a mixed bouquet of great beauty. He has made men and women of various races and nations, and when they work together as brothers in harmony, they may make a beautiful world.

In the book of Acts we read:

"And hath made of one blood all nations of men for to dwell on all the face of the earth, and hath determined the times before appointed, and the bounds of their habitation; That they should seek the Lord, if haply they might feel after him, and find him, though he be not far from every one of us; For in him we live, and move, and have our being; as certain of your own poets have said, For we are also his offspring" (17:26-28).

It is my place to be a servant among you, serving where I can, and urging you to service with me. Together we can use our offerings to help others, both at home and abroad. God help us to serve him truly.

(She takes her place with the other officers.)

Installing Official: Will the group leaders please come forward?

Group Leaders: (Place their salmon colored flowers in vase and read in unison)

We, your group leaders, promise to be faithful to the tasks assigned to us. The Book of Galatians tells us:

"And let us not be weary in well doing: for in due season we shall reap, if we faint not. As we have therefore opportunity, let us do good unto all men, especially unto them who are of the household of faith" (Gal. 6:9-10).

We trust that we may all work together for the good of all. With God's help we shall go forward in the way of the cross.

(They take their places with other officers.)

Installing Official:

Will you all bow your heads with me for the prayer of installation?

Dear heavenly Father, we come to thee this day, and present to thee these, thy children, who have undertaken new duties in thy service

for the coming year. Wilt thou have them in thy care, guiding them
in right paths and opening new avenues for service before them as
they follow the teaching of thy Son Jesus Christ.

May their willingness to undertake the responsibilities of these
offices bring them rich blessings in mental and spiritual growth, and
may we all uphold them in our prayers, encourage them by our
faithfulness, and enlarge their abilities to serve through the generosity of our hearts. Do thou now bless this service of installation, that it
may be meaningful for us all. In Jesus' name we ask it. Amen.

Hymn: "Close to Thee"

Installing Official: May we now stand and repeat the Mizpah
benediction together?

"The Lord watch between me and thee, when we are absent one from
another" (Gen. 31:49). Amen.

Installing Officers of Women's Organizations

Service 3

Materials Needed, and Instruction for Their Use:
   1 small table, covered by a cloth
   1 tall (9″ or 12″) white candle in holder, lit on table
   4 small (6″) white candles
   4 circles of cardboard, cut to hold small candles so no wax will drip
   4 file cards with officer's responses printed on them

The six-inch candles are pushed through the hole formed by the cuts
in the circles of cardboard.

Installing Official: We will pause now to install the women of the
_____ organization. We have four officers to
install. The president _____, the
secretary, _____, the vice president _____
_____, and the treasurer _____.
Will they now please come forward to be installed?

Installing Official: Here before you is a tall white candle, which

99

represents our Lord Jesus Christ. The light from his life and teaching has shone across the centuries.

"Then spake Jesus again unto them, saying, I am the light of the world: he that followeth me shall not walk in darkness, but shall have the light of life" (John 8:12).

I challenge you all to walk in that light!

President: (Lights her candle from the Christ candle, and holds it before her)

I will try to light the candle of my spirit and keep it burning by following the teaching of our Lord Jesus Christ.

"If we say that we have fellowship with him, and walk in darkness, we lie, and do not the truth. But if we walk in the light, as he is in the light, we have fellowship with one another and the blood of Jesus Christ his Son cleanseth us from all sin" (1 John 1:6-7).

As your president, I will strive to walk in the light and lead you in fellowship with each other, and in the love of God.

Vice President: (Lights her candle from Christ candle and holds it before her)

I, too, light my candle from the light that Jesus set shining. He told us:

"I am come a light into the world, that whosoever believeth in me should not abide in darkness" (John 12:46).

As your vice president, it shall be my task to lend support to our president, to preside over meetings when she is absent, and to give my encouragement to everything she undertakes. This I now pledge to do.

Secretary: (Lights candle from Christ candle, and holds it before her)

A candle flame is small, yet how it draws our eyes and our attention!

"This then is the message we have heard of him, and declare unto you, that God is light, and in him is no darkness at all" (1 John 1:5).

As your secretary it will be my task to keep membership records, send letters, and keep minutes of business meetings. I will try to do all this to the very best of my ability.

Treasurer: (Lights candle from Christ candle, and holds it before her)

The true light of God shines on everything, and the things we do are very clear to him.

"Again, a new commandment I write unto you, which thing is true in him and in you: because the darkness is past, and the true light now shineth" (1 John 2:8).

As your treasurer I will be handling the things of this world; receiving the offerings, drawing the checks, and keeping careful financial records. May God help me to do this well.

Installing Official: "He that saith he is in the light, and hateth his brother, is in darkness even until now.

He that loveth his brother abideth in the light, and there is none occasion of stumbling in him" (1 John 2:9-10).

May this truly be a year of love and light.

Installing Official: I do now pronounce you duly installed as officers of the _____ organization. May God add his blessing to each one of you. Amen.

(At this point the regular service or program may resume.)

Installing Officers of Men's Organizations

Service 1

Senior Minister (or installing official) presiding: A complete service

Men of Action

Materials Needed and Instructions for Their Use:

    President—A gavel
    Vice President—The gavel passed from the president
    Recording Secretary—A notebook
    Corresponding Secretary—A pen
    Treasurer—A wallet
    Program Chairman—A Bible

Worship Chairman—A cross

Service Chairman—A large can of fruit juice

Pianist—A large musical note made from construction paper

File cards for each officer, on which are printed the pledges they will repeat.

Give the proper symbol and file card to each officer ahead of time.

Hymn: "Rise Up, O Men of God"

Call to Worship:

"O come, let us worship and bow down: let us kneel before the Lord our maker. For he is our God; and we are the people of his pasture and the sheep of his hand" (Ps. 95:6-7).

Scripture Reading: 1 Corinthians 13

Prayer:

Almighty God, we come to thee asking that thou wilt bless our meeting together, and particularly bless these men who have accepted the responsibility of leading us in the year ahead. As our Father, Thou art aware of our doubts of our own abilities, and the questions we all have when we accept positions of trust. Thou knowest that these officers approach their offices with hesitation, as well as willingness to serve. Wilt thou grant them wisdom and courage, and give us all the will and loyalty to follow them. We would now remember those who are unable to be with us because of illness or trouble, and we ask that thou wilt touch their lives with thy hope and thy healing. Bless our church, and help us all to serve this community, and as we are able, to reach out with thy saving word to all the world. This we ask in the name of thy Son and our Master, Jesus. Amen.

Anthem or Solo: "I'm a Pilgrim"—Johnson

The Message: (by guest speaker or minister)

Men of Action!

(Notes which may be helpful in preparation)

This is a time for men of action!

To listen to the Scripture when it is read, and approve its purpose and aim is very easy.

In the Bible we read that outsiders, listening to the early apostles said: "And when they found them not, they drew Jason and certain brethren unto the rulers of the city, crying, These that have turned the world upside down are come hither also'' (Acts:17:6).

It is our task to "turn the world upside down" in our day.

Instead of hating, we are to "love our enemies."

Instead of cursing in return, we are to "bless them that curse you."

Instead of retaliating, "An eye for an eye," we are told "that ye resist not evil."

Indeed if we, as men of action, live up to our Christian teaching, we will turn our little corner of the world upside down, just as the early apostles did theirs.

Hymn: "Onward Christian Soldiers"

Installing Official: Will the officers to be installed come forward and take their places, facing the congregation, and make their pledges as I call their names?

_____ , your new president.

President: (Holds gavel out for all to see)

The gavel represents the office to which I have been elected. I promise that I will use this authority with restraint, and I will try to work with you, that together we may grow in the church. The Letter of James tells us:

"But be ye doers of the word, and not hearers only, deceiving your own selves" (1:22).

I would ask that we together may accept this verse as our motto for the year ahead, and I trust that we may all be doers, as well as hearers.

Installing Official: _____ , your new vice president.

Vice President: (Accepts the gavel which the president hands to him)

As you can see, our president has handed me the gavel, signifying that we will share the responsibilities this year. I now hold the gavel as a symbol that I will wield it and preside over meetings when the president is absent. I will encourage and support our president, and so I now return the gavel to him (returns gavel to president).

"Bear ye one another's burdens, and so fulfil the law of Christ" (Gal. 6:2).

103

May we all prove to be doers together this year.

Installing Official: _____, your new recording secretary.

Recording Secretary: I pledge, as your recording secretary, that I will keep accurate records, call the roll, and always be aware of those who are absent for one reason or another. I hold a notebook, symbol of my office (holds for all to see), and I pledge that I will do my job with care, and serve faithfully in the office you have given me.

"I have no greater joy than to hear that my children walk in truth. Beloved, thou doest faithfully whatsoever thou doest to the brethren, and to strangers" (3 John 4-5).

We read this in a letter of the beloved apostle John. May you be able to say this about me this year.

Installing Official: _____, your new corresponding secretary.

Corresponding Secretary: The pen (holding it high) represents the strength of the written word, which has been called "mightier than the sword." I vow to be true to the task given me, taking care of the correspondence of the _____ organization, in a responsible manner. Paul wrote,

"Ye are our epistle written in our hearts, known and read of all men: Forasmuch as ye are manifestly declared to be the epistle of Christ, ministered by us, written not with ink, but with the Spirit of the living God; not in tables of stone, but in fleshy tables of the heart" (2 Cor. 3:2-3).

I pledge this year to be a doer.

Installing Official: _____, your new treasurer.

Treasurer: This wallet (holding it up for all to see) represents the offerings for which I, as your treasurer, will be responsible. I pledge that I will handle carefully the funds of our organization, and I will practice integrity, but I will also remember that:

"Every man according as he purposeth in his heart, so let him give; not grudgingly, or of necessity: for God loveth a cheerful giver" (2 Cor. 9:7).

That truth must be applied to our church organizations as well as to individuals. I will deal faithfully this year with our money and our charities, so help me God.

Installing Official: _____ , your new program chairman.

Program Chairman: In my hand I hold the most important book in the world—the Bible! As your program chairman I vow to try to plan programs that will challenge your minds and your hearts, always remembering that we are a church organization.

"All scripture is given by inspiration of God, and is profitable for doctrine, for reproof, for correction, for instruction in righteousness: That the man of God may be perfect, throughly furnished unto every good work" (2 Tim. 3:16-17).

This is our goal, may all members help us to achieve it.

Installing Official: _____ , your new worship chairman.

Worship Chairman: I hold before you the empty cross, symbol of the risen Christ, and through him, our own immortality.

I vow to lead you into deeper devotion to God, closer fellowship with Jesus our Lord, and a sense of adoration that will deepen our worship experience.

"We took sweet counsel together, and walked unto the house of God in company" (Ps. 55:14).

May we walk the path of worship together this year.

Installing Official: _____ , your new service/action chairman.

Service/Action Chairman: As your service/action chairman, I would remind you that this large can of fruit juice symbolizes for us some of our charitable giving. We are aware of the hunger of the world, and we try to help. I vow to lead you, this year in actions of love and charity. It shall be my task to urge upon you greater giving, greater loving, and more action: We have been told:

"My little children, let us not love in word, neither in tongue; but in deed and in truth" (1 John 3:18).

Let us all, officers and members together, be doers of the Word and not hearers only.

Installing Official: _____ , your new pianist.

Pianist: I, as your pianist, hold my symbol of a musical note. I vow to be faithful to the task entrusted to me.

"Make a joyful noise unto the Lord, all ye lands. Serve the Lord with gladness: come before his presence with singing" (Ps. 100: 1-2).

Together we will serve the Lord this year with joy.

Installing Official: Will the members of this organization who are in the congregation now please rise? Are these the men you have elected to lead you in the year to come?

Members in Unison: They are.

Installing Official: Do you now promise to support these officers with your love and your gifts in the year ahead, and will you work harmoniously with them?

Members in Unison: This we vow.

Installing Official: I now pronounce you duly installed as officers of the _____ organization for the year ahead. May God bless you all. You may now return to your seats.

Hymn: "Forward Through the Ages"

Benediction:

"Now unto him that is able to keep you from falling, and to present you faultless before the presence of his glory with exceeding joy, To the only wise God, our Saviour, be glory and majesty, dominion and power, both now and ever" (Jude 24-25).

Bless this day in Jesus' name. Amen.

Installing Officers of Men's Organizations

Service 2

The Keys of the Kingdom

Materials Needed and Instructions for Use:

A large circle of wire with open ends, to represent a giant key ring.

Keys for each officer to be installed. Tag each key with the officer's name. On the reverse side of the tag, print the name of the person from whom the key is borrowed, so that they may be properly returned later.

File cards for each officer, containing their vows.

Call to Worship:

"Behold, I stand at the door, and knock: if any man hear my voice, and open the door, I will come in to him and, will sup with him, and he with me" (Rev. 3:20).

May we unlock the secret places in our hearts and our lives, and let him in.

Hymn: "Open My Eyes That I May See"

Invocation Prayer and the Lord's Prayer:

Our Father, we come to Thee this day, asking that Thou wilt be with us in this service, and that Thou wilt open the doors of our hearts, that we may feel Thy presence. We would truly follow our Master, Thy Son Jesus Christ, and we remember that he told us:

"After this manner therefore pray ye: Our Father, which art in heaven, Hallowed be thy name. Thy kingdom come. Thy will be done in earth, as it is in heaven. Give us this day our daily bread. And forgive us our debts, as we forgive our debtors. And lead us not into temptation, but deliver us from evil: For thine is the kingdom, and the power, and the glory, for ever. Amen" (Matt. 6:9-13).

Anthem or Solo: "I'll Walk with God"—Brodszky

Scripture Reading: Matthew 16:13-19

The Message: Door of My Heart

(Notes that may be helpful in preparation)

On the "rock" of Peter's confession that Jesus was the Christ, Jesus said he would build his church.

When he gave Peter the keys to the kingdom, they were the keys that would unlock all our hearts.

Now, with the doors of our hearts open wide, we would welcome the Christ into our very beings.

The love of God may fill our unlocked hearts that we may, by loving all mankind, change the world.

107

Pastoral Prayer: Eternal and everlasting God: Thou who art the maker of the universe, yet loving Father to each one of us. We come to thee this day and ask that thou wilt truly unlock our hearts, that we may worship thee in truth and in spirit, that, being led by thee, we may learn to love our fellowmen with the undemanding and limitless love which thou hast bestowed upon us. Make us concerned for those who are troubled, or ill, or absent from our services for any other reason. Wilt thou be near to bless them, and empower the love we have for them, that they may be drawn to our fellowship, and to thee. Be with us as we install these men, thy children, and wilt thou bless them and let them feel thy presence, for we ask all these things in the name of thy Son Jesus, the Christ. Amen.

Hymn: "Higher Ground"

Installing Official: (Holding up large key ring)

As you can see, I hold in my hand a giant key ring. We all know how important keys are, both to protect our loved ones and our valuables. If you have ever forgotten your house key, or locked your keyes inside your car, you know the feeling of panic when you cannot unlock the locked door. Today I ask you to think with me that this giant key ring represents our Lord Jesus Christ, and that as we place our keys in his hands, they become important tools to unlock many doors in our world. Will the officers to be installed in the _____ _____ organization please come forward as I call their names.

Installing Official: Will _____, the new president, please come forward?

President: (Holds up key for all to see, then places it on the giant key ring)

My key represents the key to our hearts. May we this year truly unlock the door to our inner natures. May we invite our Lord Jesus to enter in.

"For we preach not ourselves, but Christ Jesus the Lord; and ourselves your servants for Jesus' sake. For God, who commanded the light to shine out of darkness, hath shined in our hearts, to give . . . the glory of God in the face of Jesus Christ. But we have this treasure in earthen vessels, that the excellency of the power may be of God, and not of us" (2 Cor. 4:5-7).

As your president, I pledge myself to lead you this year in ways of spiritual growth, a closer fellowship with each other, and a deepened concern for those in need in our world. With God's help, we shall go forward together.

Installing Official: Will _____, your new Vice President, please come forward?

Vice President: (Places his key on giant key ring)

My key represents the loyalty and support I will give to our president in his task. We must continue to study to show ourselves worthy in the worship of God. To be truly Christian demands the whole person—heart, mind, and hands for service.

"For this is the covenant that I will make with the house of Israel after those days, saith the Lord; I will put my laws into their mind and write them in their hearts; and I will be to them a God, and they shall be to me a people: And they shall not teach every man his neighbour, and every man his brother, saying, Know the Lord, for all shall know me, from the least to the greatest" (Heb. 8:10-11).

It will be my earnest effort to support our president, to preside when he is absent, and to help lead in the paths of spiritual growth. I pledge myself to serve you, with God's help.

Installing Official: Will _____, your new secretary, please come forward?

Secretary: (Places key on giant key ring)

My key unlocks the door to records, and the written word. I feel that it is important that all our records be unlocked and available to every member.

"For this cause I also suffer these things: nevertheless I am not ashamed: for I know whom I have believed, and am persuaded that he is able to keep that which I have committed unto him against that day. Hold fast the form of sound words, which thou hast heard of me, in faith and love which is in Christ Jesus" (2 Tim. 1:12-13).

Paul wrote that to Timothy, and to you I say: "Hold fast to the form of sound words," and we will work harmoniously together during this year. This I pledge, so help me God.

Installing Official: Will _____, your new treasurer, please come forward?

Treasurer: (Placing key on giant key ring)

My key unlocks the door to the treasury, and so it is important that I handle it with care: but I must also remember that generosity is one of the qualities of a true Christian.

"But lay up for yourselves treasures in heaven, where neither moth nor rust doth corrupt, and where thieves do not break through nor steal: For where your treasure is, there will your heart be also" (Matt. 6:20-21).

I will be handling the church finances, and I will strive to do so honestly and fairly. I will always remember that there are other treasures, too, and I will deal with spiritual values, with God's help.

Installing Official: Will _____, your new chairman for program and study, please come forward?

Program/Study Chairman: (Places key on giant ring)

My key unlocks wonderful doors. Together we will study the Scriptures. Together we will share worthwhile programs with guest speakers who may challenge our minds. I will try always to have good, and varied programs, interesting for all. In 1 Thessalonians, Paul said:

"And that ye study to be quiet, and to do your own business, and to work with your own hands, as we commanded you" (1 Thess. 4:11).

With God's help, I will try to work quietly this year, feeding my deep responsibility to you, and the challenge of this office you have given me.

Installing Official: Will _____, your new chairman of worship, please come forward?

Worship Chairman: (Places key on giant ring)

My key unlocks the door to our relationship with God. It will be my task to lead you all into ever deeper pathways of worship and devotion. In this I will surely need God's guidance. I would say to you in words of Scripture:

"As ye have therefore received Christ Jesus the Lord, so walk ye in him: Rooted and built in him, and stablished in the faith, as ye have been taught, abounding therein with thanksgiving" (Col. 2:6-7).

God helping us, we will worship together.

Installing Official: Will _____, your new
chairman for service/action, please come forward?

Service/Action Chairman: (Places key on giant ring)

My key represents service to others, in any form which it may take.
Our Lord gave many examples of how we should serve one another.
It will be my task to lead you in paths of charity to those in need, and
in service to all.

"All he said unto them, The kings of the Gentiles exercise lordship
over them; and they that exercise authority upon them are called
benefactors. But ye shall not be so: but he that is greatest among you,
let him be as the younger; and he that is chief, as he that doth serve.
For whether is greater, he that sitteth at meat, or he that serveth? is
not he that sitteth at meat? But I am among you as he that serveth"
(Luke 22:25-27).

If Jesus our Lord was among us as one who serves, truly we should
serve one another. I pledge myself to be as a servant among you,
urging you on to greater giving and greater serving, with God's help.

Installing Official: I hold in my hand this giant key ring containing the
keys which are so important to our growth in the Christian life. May
we long remember this symbol and strive to keep the doors of our
hearts and minds open to the service of our Lord.

Installing Official: Will the members of the _____
organization please rise? Will you promise to support these officers
with your gifts, your time, and your prayers, and will you try with
them to grow in the Christian way?

Members in Unison: We will.

Installing Official: I now pronounce you duly installed as officers of
the _____ organization. May God add his
blessing to this installation service. You may now return to your
places.

Hymn: "God Be with You Till We Meet Again"

Senior Minister: Benediction

"The grace of the Lord Jesus Christ, and the love of God, and the
communion of the Holy Ghost, be with you all. Amen" (2 Cor.
13:14). We ask this in our Master Jesus' name. Amen.

A fellowship hour may follow if desired.

Installing Officers of Men's Organizations

Service 3

Instructions:
Since the installing official will be doing the main speaking, nothing will need to be printed for the officers. Those to be installed should each carry a Bible, marked at the verses they will read. This service includes a litany with the unison response, "We thank thee, our Father."

Installing Official: We pause now in our service/program today for a brief installation service for the officers of the _____

_____ organization. It is right that we should do so, for they undertake these offices with a deep sense of responsibility to the church as well as to their organization.

Will the officers to be installed please come forward?

Installing Official: I charge you all that you accept the office to which you have been elected with loyalty, devotion, and a serious understanding of its duties. Will you _____, as the new president, promise to lead the members in study, action and fellowship? Will you grow in your own spiritual life so that you may be an example to others?

President: I will.   (Then reading from his Bible)

"O send out thy light and thy truth; let them lead me; let them bring me to thy holy hill, and to thy tabernacles" (Ps. 43:3).

Installing Official: Will you _____, as vice president, try to encourage and support your president? Will you preside when he is absent and, even more important, will you help him as he leads this organization through the coming year?

Vice President: I will.   (Then reading from his Bible)

"And let us not be weary in well doing: for in due season we shall reap, if we faint not.

As we have therefore opportunity, let us do good unto all men, especially unto them who are of the household of faith" (Gal. 6:9-10).

Installing Official: Will you _____, as the new secretary, keep accurate records of the membership and minutes of the business meetings, and always be careful for the written word? Words, spoken or written, are very important. Will you promise to use them with great care?

Secretary: I will. (Then reading from his Bible)

"That ye might walk worthy of the Lord unto all pleasing, being fruitful in every good work, and increasing in the knowledge of God; Strengthened with all might, according to his glorious power, unto all patience and longsuffering with joyfulness" (Col. 1:10-11).

Installing Official: Will you, _____, as the new treasurer promise to handle the things of this world with all diligence and honesty? Will you care for the offerings given you as treasurer, but be aware that generosity is a quality of the good Christian life?

Treasurer: I will. (Then reading from his Bible)

"But the wisdom that is from above is first pure, then peaceable, gentle, and easy to be intreated, full of mercy and good fruits, without partiality, and without hypocrisy. And the fruit of righteousness is sown in peace of them that make peace" (Jas. 3:17-18).

Installing Official: Will the members of the _____ organization, and all of those present please rise and join in the installation litany? The response will be: We thank thee, our Father.

Installing Official: For these men who have promised to serve as officers in the _____ organization

People in Unison: We thank thee, our Father.

Installing Official: Because they are willing to give of their time, their talent, and their money to thy service

People in Unison: We thank thee, our Father.

Installing Official: Because it will be their task to lead, and ours to follow. We know that with thy help they will lead well

People in Unison: We thank thee, our Father.

Installing Official: Because the fellowship of the _____ organization is a part of our local church, and even beyond that, because it is a part of thy church universal

People in Unison: We thank thee, our Father.

113

Installing Official: Will you all now bow with me for the prayer of installation?

Our Father and our God, we are thankful to thee that Thou hast brought us so far on the pilgrimage of our lives, and hast always raised up for us leaders to whom we may give honor and respect. Wilt thou truly bless these men who stand before thee, that they may lead good lives, and lead us in ways that will be pleasing in thy sight. Do thou, by thy blessing, truly install them in the places of leadership, and may they walk ever beside thee in the year ahead. We ask all this in the name of our Lord and Savior, Jesus Christ. Amen.

(At this time the regular service/program may resume.)

Installing Officers of Youth Organizations

Service 1

Images of the Eternal

Materials Needed and Instructions for Their Use:

A Styrofoam cross on a firm base.

A small table, covered with a cloth.

Seven small sprigs of some type of evergreen (pine, live oak, or any sprigs of leaves or needles which stay green all year). It is important that these be live greens, and not artificial.

Seven file cards, on which are printed the officers vows (Cut slits in the stiff Styrofoam cross, as shown on chart No. 1, so that it will be easy for the officers to insert their sprigs of evergreen in the cross.)

Call to Worship:

"Come now, and let us reason together, saith the Lord: though your sins be as scarlet, they shall be as white as snow; though they be red like crimson, they shall be as wool" (Isa. 1:18).

Hymn: "I Would Be True"

Invocation Prayer and the Lord's Prayer:

Our dear Lord and Heavenly Father, we come to thee this day, seeking thy rich blessing. We know that thou hast led us in the past,

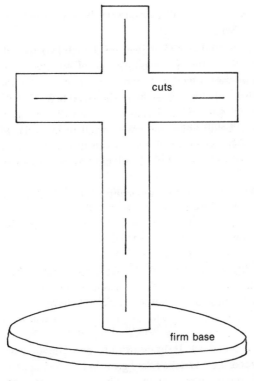

cuts

firm base

Chart No. 1

and we believe that thou wilt be with us in all of life. We would this day be particularly aware of the eternal nature of our souls—knowing that with Christ, our lives are lived here and now, and that with him we shall go on in eternal life and joy. We remember that he taught us to pray, saying:

"Our Father which art in heaven, Hallowed be thy name. Thy kingdom come. Thy will be done in earth, as it is in heaven. Give us this day our daily bread. And forgive us our debts, as we forgive our debtors. And lead us not into temptation, but deliver us from evil: For thine is the kingdom, and the power, and the glory, for ever. Amen" (Matt. 6:9-13).

Anthem or Solo: "Where The Spirit of the Lord Is"—Adams

115

Scripture Reading: 1 Corinthians 15:39-49
Message: Images of the Eternal
(Notes which may be helpful in preparation)

As we have borne the image of the earthly, we shall also bear the image of the heavenly.

Our spirit is that which came from God, and inhabits an earthly body as we inhabit a house.

It is for our spiritual nature always to control the physical, not for our earthly bodies to rule the spirit.

In our Scripture lesson for today we have a clear picture of our dual nature.

God has given us a spiritual control over the physical nature of our bodies. Let us exercise this control always.

May we always, in our dealings with others, bear the image of the eternal nature we have been granted.

Hymn: "Give Me Thy Heart"

Pastoral Prayer:

Almighty and eternal God, our hearts would be open to thy leading. Wilt thou bless these young people who have undertaken responsibilities in the church youth organization, and wilt thou be very near to them in the months ahead. Help them to be "images of the eternal" for us all. Help us all to be encouraging and supportive of their leadership, and may they grow in love and understanding of thy way as they seek to serve thee. Be thou our constant guide, that we may do and say things that are pleasing to thee. Comfort the ill with thy healing touch: bless the afflicted with thy guiding hand; care for us all as we seek to follow the path of our Master and Savior, Jesus Christ. Wilt thou grant thy blessing upon this service and lead us all, for we ask it in the name of thy Son, Jesus. Amen.

Installing Official: We come now to formally install the officers of the _____ organization. Just as the empty cross is a symbol that our Lord has been resurrected, so evergreen is a symbol of immortality and eternal life. In the Book of Galatians we read:

"But the fruit of the Spirit is love, joy, peace, longsuffering, gentleness, goodness, faith" (5:22).

These are immortal traits, and we trust that the officers which have

116

been chosen will exemplify these qualities. We are sure they will approach their tasks seriously and responsibly. Will the officers to be installed please come forward and give their vows as I call their names?

Installing Official: Will _____, your new president, please come forward?

President: I hold in my hand a piece of evergreen. How truly in all ages, evergreen has symbolized immortality—the eternal life which Christians find in Jesus Christ, our Lord. As one fruit of the Spirit, my evergreen represents love.

"Hereby perceive we the love of God, because he laid down his life for us: and we ought to lay down our lives for the brethren" (1 John 3:16).
"My little children, let us not love in word, neither in tongue; but in deed and in truth" (v. 18).

We will turn this empty cross into a living cross by placing in it this living green. (He places his evergreen in top cut in cross.) The "fruit of the Spirit" which I will try to show is love. May God help me to do my job. Amen.

Installing Official: Will _____, your new vice president, please come forward?

Vice President: I too have a piece of evergreen, the eternally green shrub and tree. The trait I will try to show in support of our president is "joy." It will be my task to preside over business meetings when the president is absent, but it will also be for me to cheerfully encourage him/her.
(Places evergreen in second cut in cross)

"If you keep my commandments, ye shall abide in my love; even as I have kept my Father's commandments, and abide in his love. These things have I spoken unto you, that my joy might remain in you, and that your joy might be full" (John 15:10-11).

Installing Official: Will _____, your new secretary please come forward?

Secretary: My share of the evergreen shrub represents "peace," and it is my hope that if there are differences between friends, I may be a peacemaker.

(Places the evergreen in third cut in cross.)

It will be my task to keep the membership records, keep the minutes of business meetings, and write all the things that need to be written for our organization. Jesus said:

"Peace I leave with you, my peace I give unto you: not as the world giveth, give I unto you.

Let not your heart be troubled, neither let it be afraid" (John 14:27).

Installing Official: Will _____, your new treasurer, please come forward?

Treasurer: This bit of evergreen represents "longsuffering," or as we would say it, patience. The Book of James tell us:

"Knowing this, that the trying of your faith worketh patience. But let patience have her perfect work, that ye may be perfect and entire, wanting nothing" (1:3-4).

(Places evergreen in fourth cut in cross)

I would be patient in dealing with our treasury and the things of this world, and honest in my accounting. I know that patience is a difficult virtue, particularly for the young, and so I will ask God to help me this year that I may really learn patience.

Installing Official: Will _____, your new chairman of worship, please come forward?

Chairman of Worship: Worship is the very foundation for all religious growth, and so I will place my evergreen nearest the base of the cross.

(Places evergreen in lowest cut on cross.)

My piece of evergreen represents "gentleness," and so I will try to gently uphold our spiritual growth.

"But the hour cometh, and now is, when the true worshippers shall worship the Father in spirit and in truth: for the Father seeketh such to worship him. God is a Spirit: and they that worship him must worship him in spirit and in truth" (John 4:23-24).

I will truly seek to lead our worship, that it may be in spirit and in truth.

Installing Official: Will _____, your new chairman for program and study, please come forward?

Chairman of Program/Study: The programs we will have and the study we will undertake are very important, and I feel that my task is a very responsible one. I might even say that it is like "a good right arm," and so I will place my evergreen in the right arm of our empty cross.

(Places evergreen in cut at right end of cross.)

My evergreen represents "goodness," and goodness comes only through serious study, and programs that have meaning for us. Psalm 139 tells us:

"Search me, O God, and know my heart: try me, and know my thoughts: And see, if there be any wicked way in me, and lead me in the way everlasting" (vv. 23-24).

Installing Official: Will _____, your new chairman for recreation and action, please come forward?

Chairman for Recreation/Action: Mine is a twofold task. I am to plan recreation for our organization—and social recreation is a real part of our Christian fellowship. I am also to plan ways in which we can help others—our action in charity and love. My piece of evergreen represents "faith," and it will be the final bit of evergreen that changes an empty cross into a living cross.

(Places evergreen in slot on left arm of cross.)

"Above all things, have fervent charity among yourselves: for charity shall cover the multitude of sins. Use hospitality one to another without grudging. As every man hath received the gift, even so minister the same one to another, as good stewards of the manifold grace of God" (1 Pet. 4:8-10).

And so I would urge charity, that the grace of God may be ours this year.

Installing Official: Will everyone please rise?
Do you accept these dedicated young officers to lead the _____ _____ organization of the church, and do you promise them your encouragement and support?

People in Unison: We do!

Installing Official: I now pronounce the officers of the _____ _____ organization duly installed, and may God add his rich blessing to this service. You may be seated.

119

Hymn: "Faith Is the Victory"
Benediction:

"Now the Lord of peace himself give you peace always by all means. The Lord be with you all" (2 Thess. 3:16). In Jesus' name. Amen.

Installing Officers of Youth Organizations

Service 2

Biblical Profiles in Courage

Materials Needed:

File cards for each officer to be installed, with biographical sketches from Scriptures. They should be given out before the program/service begins.

Call to Worship:

"Be strong and of good courage, fear not, nor be afraid of them: for the Lord thy God, he it is that doth go with thee; he will not fail thee, nor forsake thee" (Deut. 31:6).

Hymn: "Mine Eyes Have Seen the Glory"
Invocation Prayer:

Almighty and omnipotent God, we approach thy presence this day and invoke thy Spirit in this place. Wilt thou grant us the courage that finds itself in gentleness, and is made perfect in humility. Bless this service, and we who wait in thy holy presence, for we ask it in the name of our Lord, Jesus Christ. Amen.

Anthem or Solo: "The Lord's Prayer"—Malotte
Scripture Reading: Ephesians 6:10-18
Message: Qualities of Courage

(Notes which may be helpful in preparation)

If we chose qualities of courage, we might say one must be big and strong—but the Scriptures tell us to be strong in the Lord, and in his power.

Our armor is to include truth and righteousness. These are the qualities that give us power and strength.

If we were preparing for battle, would we feel that the qualities of peace and faith were necessary? Yet the Scriptures tell us they must be a part of our armor.

Then finally we need to take the sword of the "Spirit," which is the word of God.

If we are praying always, and these qualities are in us and abound, we shall be ready for any trouble the world may bring.

Hymn: "Sitting at the Feet of Jesus"

Installing Official: We come now to that part of our service/program where we shall formally install the officers of the _____ _____ organization. Sometime before he was elected President of the United States, John F. Kennedy wrote a book entitled *Profiles in Courage.* We would like, today, to consider some of the biblical profiles in courage which we find in the Scriptures. We could have chosen to speak of Abraham, Noah, Moses, Daniel, and David—those well-known courageous leaders. Instead, we have chosen to speak of lesser known men and women who exhibited courage of many kinds.

Installing Official: Will_____, the new president, please come forward?

President: In the time of Deborah, Israel was in bondage, and the captain of the enemy army was named Sisera. Deborah was a judge, or ruler in Israel.

When she ordered the captain of her army, Barak, to fight Sisera, he replied that he would do so only if she, Deborah would lead the Israelite army.

So, like Joan of Arc, in a later century, Deborah led the army of her nation to victory over their oppressors (Judg. 4:4-9). As your president, I will remember Deborah, and be ready to lead wherever the path may take me. I believe God will give me the courage I need.

Installing Official: Will_____, the new vice president please come forward?

Vice President: We all know that Stephen was the first Christian martyr. Stephen preached a sermon, that so angered the officials that they stoned him to death. It took great courage for this young deacon to stand before a hostile crowd and preach about his Lord, Jesus, the Christ. It took great courage for Stephen to accept, without returning violence for violence, the pain of being stoned to death. How

121

Christlike he was, saying, "Lay not this sin to their charge!" (Acts 7:60). May I, as I help and support our president, have the kind of courage Stephen showed, and so practice gentleness and patience in all that I do. With God's help, I will serve you with courage.

Installing Official: Will_____, your new secretary, please come forward?

Secretary: Esther was an ancient Jewish queen of Persia. Yet not even the queen dared to approach the king unless he sent for her. The penalty for approaching unbidden could be death. When Queen Esther approached the king to plead for her people, she took her life in her hands. She said: "If I perish, I perish" (Esther 4:16). If the king had placed the sharp end of his scepter toward her, she would have been sentenced to death. But he held it out to her top first. Because she had courage, she was able to save herself and her people. May I have quiet courage in life, and be willing to take risks, in order to grow in my Christian life. I will pray God to help me with my task as secretary, this year.

Installing Official: Will _____, your new treasurer, please come forward?

Treasurer: Nathan, the ancient prophet, showed great courage when he stood before David, the powerful king, and placed his life on the line. It was after David had deliberately ordered the husband of Bathsheba sent into the front line of battle so that he would be killed, and David could then marry his widow. The prophet Nathan told David a story of two men, one rich with great flocks of sheep, his neighbor poor, owning only one poor little lamb. When the rich man had company, instead of killing a sheep from his flocks, he took the poor man's lamb and cooked it for his guest. When David, horrified, denounced that action, "Thou art the man!" Nathan said (2 Sam. 12:7).

And David realized Nathan had been telling him the story of his own treatment of Bathsheba's husband! David could have had Nathan executed for this terrible denunciation. Instead, David repented, and was sorry for his sin. Courage is a wonderful thing. I hope that I, too, will have the courage to stand for the right, as I serve as one of your leaders, this year.

Installing Official: Will _____, your new chairman for worship, please come forward?

Chairman for Worship: I would tell you of two men of courage, and how because they were helpers and encouragers, they saved the day for Israel. I, too, would be a helper and encourager of our officers. When Joshua fought Amalek, long ago, they found that while Moses held his hands up toward God, holding his rod, the Israelite army prevailed. But when Moses became exhausted, and lowered his arms with the rod, the Amalakites began to win.

Seeing the problem, Aaron and Hur came to stand on either side of Moses, and held up his hands all day till the sun went down (Ex. 17:12). And, so, the Israelites won the battle. How very important to leaders are those who lend support! May I have the courage to make our worship moments meaningful to us all through this year.

Installing Official: Will _____, your new chairman for program/study please come forward?

Chairman for Program/Study: Ruth, a girl of Moab, showed a great deal of courage as well as love and compassion. When she, her sister-in-law, and mother-in-law were all left widows, the other girl returned to her own family, but Ruth chose to stay with her mother-in-law and to care for her.

"Intreat me not to leave thee; . . . thy people shall be my people, and thy God my God," Ruth told her mother-in-law (Ruth 1:16). She left her own country to return to Israel with her mother-in-law, because she loved her and had compassion for her in the loss of her sons. This took great courage. May our studies and special programs help us to grow in the same Christian attributes: love, compassion, and courage.

Installing Official: Will _____, your new chairman for action/recreation, please come forward?

Chairman for Action/Recreation: Perhaps one of the most difficult things in the world is to make up with a friend after a deep quarrel. John Mark apparently had the courage to continue to seek to heal the difference he had with the apostle Paul, until at last they were reconciled. On one of the missionary journeys, young Mark left the others and went home (Acts:13:13). Some time later when Barnabas would have taken Mark with them, Paul disagreed, and so they parted. Barnabas and John Mark went one way; Paul and Silas went another (Acts 15:37-38).

Still John Mark and Paul must have reconciled, for we read in Paul's later letter to Timothy: "Take Mark, and bring him with thee; for he is profitable to me for the ministry" (2 Tim. 4:11). Surely the courage to become reconciled with an estranged friend is something that we all need! May we remember young John Mark, and may the actions that we take be done with that kind of quiet courage. My task will be to lead in actions of service to others, and also to plan social affairs which may deepen our fellowship. May I do it well!

Installing Official: I now pronounce you duly installed as officers of the _____ organization. May you remember these biblical profiles in courage, and may you, too, live your lives with courage.

I trust that you will have the boldness of Deborah, the love and compassion of Ruth, the honesty of Nathan, the cheerful encouragement of Aaron and Hur, the devotion of Esther, the peace of Stephen, and the spiritual courage and endurance that made Paul and Mark continue to seek friendship.

May God richly bless you all with Christan qualities of service and love. In Jesus' name. Amen.

Hymn: "Stand Up, Stand Up for Jesus"

Benediction:

"Peace be to the brethren, and love with faith, from God the Father and the Lord Jesus Christ.

Grace be to all them that love our Lord Jesus Christ in sincerity. Amen" (Eph. 6:23-24).

A time of fellowship may follow

Installing Officers of Youth Organizations

Service 3

Installing Official: We come now to the time for installation of the officers in the _____ organization. Will the officers to be installed please come forward and stand before us? (He/she then addresses each officer in turn.)

Installing Official: You _____, as president of the _____ organization, will have the task of leading your friends in Christian growth.

"Have I not commanded thee? Be strong and of good courage; be not afraid, neither be thou dismayed: for the Lord thy God is with thee whithersoever thou goest" (Josh. 1:9).

Will you always remember that this is so, that the Lord is with you in all you do? Do you willingly accept this office and pledge yourself to lead to the best of your ability, with God's help?

President: I do.

Installing Official: You, _____, have been chosen as vice president of the _____ organization. This means that you must cheerfully serve with your president. You will preside over business meetings when the president is absent.

"Even the youths shall faint and be weary, and the young men shall utterly fall: But they that wait upon the Lord shall renew their strength; they shall mount up with wings as eagles; they shall run, and not be weary; and they shall walk and not faint" (Isa. 40:30-31).

Do you promise to encourage true Christian living, so that indeed all may mount up with wings as eagles? Do you accept the office of vice president, and vow to be a true leader?

Vice President: I do.

Installing Official: You, _____, have been chosen as secretary of the _____ organization. It will be your task to keep membership records and also the minutes of business meetings.

"Wherefore, I also, after I heard of your faith in the Lord Jesus, and love unto all the saints, Cease not to give thanks for you, making mention of you in my prayers; That the God of our Lord Jesus Christ, the Father of glory, may give unto you the spirit of wisdom and revelation in the knowledge of him" (Eph. 1:15-17).

Do you undertake your task of leadership with serious understanding, and with God's help do you here promise to do your best, and to grow in your Christian life?

Secretary: I do.

Installing Official: Will_____ please respond, as you have been chosen treasurer of the _____ _____ organization? The task you deal with has to do with the

125

treasures of this world. To this task you must bring the qualities of honesty, generosity, and a close attention to detail, in keeping the records of your office.

"For God, who commanded the light to shine out of darkness, hath shined in our hearts, to give the light of the knowledge of the glory of God in the face of Jesus Christ. But we have this treasure in earthen vessels, that the excellency of the power may be of God, and not of us" (2 Cor. 4:6-7).

Do you promise always to remember that our treasures are in earthen vessels, that whatever we do, it may be done for the glory of God, and not for our own advancement or pride, truly for the glory of God the Father? Do you vow to use this office with integrity.

Treasurer: I do.

Installing Official: Will the people now here assembled please rise? Do you, the members of the _____ organization, and the members of this congregation now declare that you will support these officers through the coming year? Do you promise that you will cheerfully support them with your time, your money, and your prayers, in the tasks they may undertake?

People in Unison: We do.

Installing Official: I now pronounce you duly installed as officers in the _____ organization. As your very first act of office, will you bow with all of us in prayer for God's blessing?

Installation Prayer:

Our Father, we ask that thou wilt most truly bless these young people who have solemnly accepted leadership among their friends, in order that all may grow in their love for thee. Wilt thou place thy hand upon them, that they may feel thy presence, and be strengthened in the things they say and do. May all be done to thy honor and glory, for we ask it in thy Son's name, Jesus our Lord. Amen.

A fellowship hour may follow.

PART 5
AREA OF COMMUNITY
FELLOWSHIP

This section of the book deals with community organizations which may be searching for services that will add dignity to the office and to the officers elected.

As with all the previous services, the installing official should feel free to choose as little or as much as desired.

It is our hope that these services/programs may be adapted for many uses, from children's clubs to adult social clubs; veteran's organizations, or even to officers in a board of directors when more formality is desired for their installation.

We do not in these cases use Scriptures, and these are therefore briefer services, and use less symbols. There is more formality in all but those planned for social clubs.

It is our understanding that most civic organizations have their own ritual for installation of officers, but nevertheless one brief service of installation has been included, in case it is desired.

As we close this book of installation services, we hope that it will serve a real need, that its purpose may be fulfilled.

Installing Officers in a Civic Organization

Service 1

America Always!

Materials Needed, and Instructions for Their Use:

A large Styrofoam base (may be taped to table for stability)

A small table

Two five-inch circles cut from white poster board, on which is drawn the symbol for the organization, or the initials of the club's name (as Community Brotherhood Club)

An American flag on a stick

Two ten-inch, thin dowel sticks

Place the American flag in the center of the base. On either side, place small dowel sticks, with poster board circles taped to their tops, as in chart No. 1

The outgoing president should preside over the first part of this service.

Song By All: "Mine Eyes Have Seen the Glory"

Pledge of Allegiance to the Flag: Led by the outgoing president.

Prayer: (By outgoing chaplain)

Creator God, thou hast led us through another year. We thank thee for thy guidance, and we ask for thy care in the year ahead. Bless our organization, our community, and our nation, that we may be truly "one nation under God." Amen.

Outgoing President: I wish to speak for all my fellow officers who are retiring from office. It has been a real privilege and a challenge to serve as your president, and I shall always remember the loyal support I received from the other officers and from the members. May we have a rich and rewarding year ahead under the officers whom you have elected.

Solo: "The Star Spangled Banner"—Key

The Message: We Love America!

(Notes which may be helpful to the speaker)

Review the principles on which the organization is founded, serving veterans, or the community as a whole.

As we cherish our freedoms, our love for our country deepens.

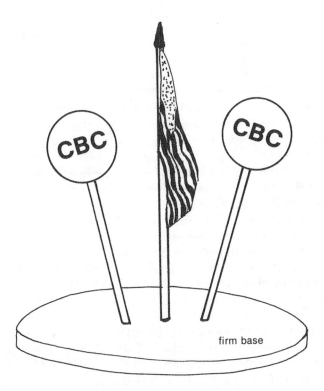

Chart No. 1

Let us remind ourselves of the great values written into our Constitution, and even more deeply written in our hearts.

Outgoing President: At this time I would call upon _____
_____, who is to be our installing official.

Installing Official: To you, _____, retiring president of the _____ organization, we want to offer the sincere thanks of all the membership for the job you have done. You and your fellow officers have led us willingly, loyally, and courageously, and we give you our deepest thanks. (He shakes hands with the outgoing president, who then takes his place in the audience.)

Installing Official: As I call their names, will the officers to be installed please come forward and face the members?

Your new president _____

Your new vice president _____

Your new secretary _____

Your new treasurer _____

Your new chaplain _____

Installing Official: Will all the members please stand? Are these the persons you have chosen to be your officers, and to lead you through this next year?

People in Unison: They are.

Installing Official: Will you now pledge to these officers your support in all ways, with your time, with your interest, and with your money in the projects they may undertake?

People in Unison: We will.

Installing Official: You may now be seated, as the officers take their vows. Will you, _____ as the new president, vow to uphold the principles of this organization? Will you serve the members, the community, and the nation faithfully and honorably, fulfilling all the duties of the office to which you have been elected?

President: I will.

Installing Official: Will you _____, as the new vice president, try always to support and help the president in his/her leadership task? Will you preside at business meetings when he/she is absent, and be loyal to all the projects undertaken during this year?

Vice President: I will.

Installing Official: Will you, _____, as the new secretary, promise to be faithful to the duties given you? Will you keep accurate membership rolls, take minutes at business meetings, and have charge of the correspondence necessary to your office? Will you pledge to carry out these tasks to the best of your ability?

Secretary: I will.

Installing Official: Will you, _____, as the new treasurer, pledge to fulfill the office with care and integrity? Will you keep accurate financial records, make regular reports, and be supportive of the president, and in all ways be loyal to this organization?

Treasurer: I will.

Installing Official: Will you, _____, as the

new chaplain, accept the spiritual oversight of the membership? Will you be available for counseling, and lead not only in prayer, but in kindness and courtesy, so that you will be an example in fellowship?

Chaplain: I will.

Installing Official: I now pronounce that you are duly installed as the new officers of the _____ organization. May you lead all the members in a challenging and growing year.

Song in Unison: "God Bless America"—Berlin

Newly Installed Chaplain: God bless us every one! Amen.

A social hour may follow if desired.

Installing Officers in a Civic Organization

Service 2

Materials Needed and Instruction for Use:

A small, cloth-covered table

A vase holding evergreen branches on table (or place a large evergreen branch on table)

Installing Official: In ancient Greece and Rome, evergreen wreaths of laurel leaves were placed upon the heads of their heroes to signify immortality. We have placed here on the table evergreen, which to us symbolizes the fact that we will long remember the service our officers have given this past year, and that we look forward to the leadership which our newly elected officers will furnish during the year to come. We now have a double duty. It is our privilege to express our gratitude to the officers who have served us so well and faithfully. Will the members please stand and express their thanks by generous applause?

Outgoing President: On behalf of all the retiring officers, I want to accept your thanks, and assure you that it has been a pleasure and a privilege to serve you. (He then returns to his place in the audience.)

Installing Official: The second part of my duty is to install the officers you have chosen to serve in this coming year. Will the following officers please come forward and face the members, as I call your names?

The new president _____

The new vice president _____

The new secretary _____

The new treasurer _____

Installing Official: (To the membership)

Do you, the members of the _____ organiza-
tion, pledge your friendship and loyal support to these officers, and
do you promise to follow their leadership during the coming year?

Members in Unison: We do.

Installing Official: Do you, the newly elected officers of the _____
_____ organization, promise to be faithful to the
duties of the office to which you have been elected: Do you vow to
do your best to lead the members in a worthy manner, and to be loyal
in word and deed?

New Officers in Unison: We do.

Installing Official: I now pronounce that you are duly installed as
officers of the _____ organization, and may
the year ahead be one of growth and achievement.

At this time the regular program of the meeting may resume.

Installing Officers in a Civic Organization

Service 3

Material Needed and Instructions for Use:

A gavel, or very large key (or one cut from poster board)

Installing Official: We come now in our program to a part which is
solemn, yet joyous. At this time we must say our farewells and thank
yous to the fine officers who have served this organization so well
during this past year. We owe a debt of gratitude to them, and words
are very inadequate to express that debt. We are here also to install
those officers who have been elected and have agreed to serve you in
the year to come. So it is truly a time of "Hail and Farewell!" Will
_____, the outgoing president, please come

forward to represent all those officers who have served with him/her? (The installing official hands the gavel or large key, symbol of office, to the outgoing president.) Will _____, the new president, please come forward?

Installing Official: (to outgoing president)

To you, _____, as the representative for those others who have served with you in leadership positions, we offer the gratitude and friendship of every member for your tireless efforts on our behalf. This gavel (or key) is a symbol of your authority, and I now ask that you face your successor, and repeat after me:

"I, president of _____, now bequeath to you, _____, this gavel (or key) and the duties of the office of president. I charge you to use this symbol, and your office, with loyalty and good faith."

(The president-elect accepts the gavel [or key] and they shake hands. The outgoing president returns to his seat.)

Installing Official: Will you, _____, our new president, please repeat after me,

"I, _____, accept this gavel (or key) and the office it represents with a deep sense of honor and responsibility. I will strive to serve faithfully and well. I will try to be available to members at all times, and I will attempt to lead to the best of my ability. This I vow to all."

Installing Official: Will you now turn and face the members as they make their pledge to you? Please rise to repeat your pledge to our president.

Installing Official: Will you now pledge to support _____, your new president, and give him/her your loyalty and friendship? Will you try to carry out the programs and activities which he/she may initiate during the year?

Members in Unison: We will.

Installing Official: I now invite the following officers to join their president.

The vice president _____
Recording secretary _____

133

Corresponding secretary _____

Treasurer _____

Membership chairman _____

Activities chairman _____

(or whatever titles are used for the various offices.)

Installing Official: Will you promise faithfully to fulfill the duties of the office to which you have been elected, and to support your president in the task he/she has undertaken?

Will you serve the membership of _____ and do your best to be worthy leaders?

Officers in Unison: We will.

Installing Official: Will you, the members of this organization solemnly pledge that you will support these officers that you have elected? Will you work when called upon, and try to make this an outstanding year in your organization?

Members in Unison: We will.

Installing Official: I now declare you duly installed as officers of the _____ organization, and congratulate you upon the offices you have accepted. The membership is to be congratulated upon the officers they have chosen. Have a wonderful year.

At this point the regular program could resume.

Installing Officers in a Social Club

Service 1

Materials needed and Instruction for Their Use:

A small table

A large 15-inch circle cut from white poster board

A 12-inch triangle cut from white poster board

A 12-inch Styrofoam base, with cut in which to place triangle

A package of brightly colored balloons, inflated and tied

Place the large cardboard circle on table, with Styrofoam base in

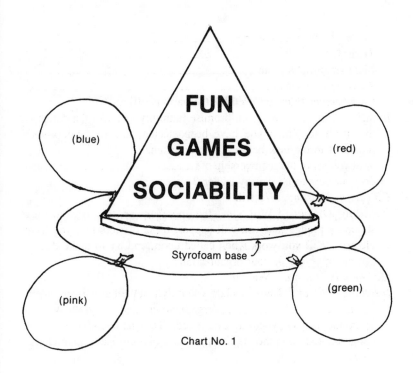

FUN

GAMES

SOCIABILITY

(blue)

(red)

(pink)

(green)

Styrofoam base

Chart No. 1

center, and the triangle with words *FUN, GAMES,* and *SOCIABILITY* printed on it, placed in the cut in Styrofoam.

Tape four inflated balloons in suggested colors onto rim of poster board.

Inflate all the balloons in package, and hang from strings to decorate the hall.

Sing-Along: (Directed by recreation chairman, or the outgoing president) Use old familiar songs that all will sing—

"Down By the Old Millstream"
"Goodnight Sweetheart"
"I Love You Truly"
and rounds such as:

"Row, Row, Row Your Boat"
"Are You Sleeping, Brother John?"

Here a humorous reading may be used, such as the following.

Radio Mix-Up

In the early days of radio, when crystal sets were used, it was often difficult to get one station and block out others. Sometimes two stations would fade in and out, mixing the programs in ways that were confusing, and many times funny.

The young bride had asked her husband to listen to the radio recipe given by a famous chef. He did his very best, and copied every word, but two stations interfered with each other, one giving the recipe, the other an exercise class.

When the young husband read to his bride what he had copied, this is what he had written:

Hands on hips, place one cup of flour on shoulders, raise knees and depress toes, and wash thoroughly in one-half cup of milk.

In four counts raise both legs and mash two hard boiled eggs in a sieve. Repeat six times. Inhale one teaspoon of baking powder and one cup of flour, breathe through the nose and exhale and sift.

Attention: jump to a stride stand, and bend the white of an egg backward and forward overhead, and in four counts make a stiff dough that will stretch at the waist. Lie flat on the floor and roll into a marble the size of a walnut.

Hop backward and forward in boiling water, but do not boil into a stationary run afterward. In ten minutes remove from the fire and dry with a towel. Breathe deeply, put on a bathrobe, and serve with fish soup.

Announcements and Introduction of Guests
Outgoing President: Introduction of guest speaker.
The Message: Life Should Be Bright
            (Notes which may be helpful in preparation)

Life is made up of many varied sides.

There is the serious side, where we face our problems, earn our living, and get our education.

There is the emotional side, where we fall in love, marry, and raise our families.

There is the intellectual side, where we need to keep studying, seeking, and growing all our lives.

But there is also the social side, where we need companionship, good fellowship, and recreation to balance the other levels of life.

Our organization is a social one, and it fulfills a real need in our lives. It is a place to form friendships, to relax and to laugh together.

Let us remember that laughter and enjoyment are an important part of our lives, and let us cherish the ability to see the funny side of things.

Installing Official: We come now in our program to the place where we will install the officers to serve in the coming year. We would take this opportunity to express our thanks to those officers who have served us so faithfully and well this past year. In a social club, it is important to have officers who are faithful to their tasks. Without plans for programs, our club would be much the poorer: and to have these plans, there must be business meetings where plans may be discussed.

At this time I would ask, _____ , your new president to come forward and face the members.

Installing Official: Will you, _____ , now elected as our president, accept willingly the duties imposed upon you? Will you strive to encourage fellowship and friendship, remembering to keep the programs light and relaxing? Will you preside over business meetings and make the decisions that need to be made in this coming year?

President: I will.

Installing Official: Will you, _____ , now elected as our vice president, take a similar vow? Willyou preside at business meetings when the president is absent, encourage sociability and friendliness? Will you try to support the president in all that he/she attempts to do?

Vice President: I will.

Installing Official: Will you, _____ , elected as our new secretary, pledge to keep accurate membership records, carry on correspondence, and the various duties of a secretary? In a social club, the duties of a secretary are very important. Will you pledge to fulfill those duties to the best of your ability?

Secretary: I will.

Installing Official: Will you, _____ , our new treasurer, now give your pledge? Will you keep honest and careful financial records, draw checks when needed, and do all those things which come under the responsibility of "treasurer" Will you promise to fulfill the task with loyalty and integrity?

Treasurer: I will.

Installing Official: Will the members please stand and make their pledge to these newly elected officers?

Will you pledge to give these officers your friendship, support them with your dues and offerings, and willingly give time to make this social club one where harmony and good fellowship rule?

Members in Unison: We will.

Installing Official: Pronouncement

By the giving and receiving of these pledges between officers and members, I now declare that the new officers of the _____ _____ organization are duly installed.

May this be a year of growth and enjoyment.

At this time, the strings holding the balloons should be cut, and whatever the usual social time enjoyed by members should be held.

Installing Officers in a Social Club

Service 2

Installing Official: At this place in our program, we would pause to formally install the officers who will lead us in the coming year. As I name them, will the officers who who were elected come forward and stand facing the membership?

The new president _____

The new vice president _____

The new secretary _____

138

The new treasurer _____

The new pianist _____

Installing Official: Will you, the newly elected officers of the _____
_____ organization, now promise faithfully to carry
out the duties of your several offices? Will you be loyal to the aims
of our club, and careful in carrying out your tasks?

Officers in Unison: We will.

Installing Official: Will the members please stand and repeat their
vow to the officers? Will you, the members, promise to preserve the
friendships made in this social club, and to support these, your
officers, as they strive to carry on the work of the club this coming
year?

Members in Unison: We will.

Installing Official: With the giving and receiving of these formal
vows, I now pronounce the officers of the _____
_____ organization duly installed, and may you have a fine year
ahead.

The regular social program of the organization will resume at this time.